T0089043

Praise for *Obliquity* by John Kay

"Provocative, profound, and counterintuitive."
—*The Wall Street Journal*

"*Obliquity* is a characteristic John Kay production. It is a pleasure to read." —*Financial Times*

"One of our cleverest thinkers." —*The Independent* (London)

"[A] smart, witty book." —*London Evening Standard*

"His book pushes the boundaries of business, flirting with chaos theory. Still, his argument is anchored in a string of concrete examples that reflect his scope." —*The Age* (Melbourne)

"How rare it is for an academic economist to write with such clarity, intelligence, and courage." —The *Spectator* (UK)

"*Obliquity* is a great read even for those who do not have much of a background in business and economics, and a worthy addition to the series of pop economics books such as *The Undercover Economist* and *Freakonomics*." —*Daily News & Analysis* (India)

"John Kay is an admirable debunker of myths and false beliefs— he can see substantial things others don't. Read this book."
—Nassim Taleb, professor of risk engineering at New York University and author of *The Bed of Procrustes*, *The Black Swan*, and *Fooled by Randomness*

"In a book that is witty, wise, and a pleasure to read, John Kay shows convincingly that most of us take the wrong approach to making our biggest decisions—in work and in life. Take this book to heart and your decision making will be changed forever."

— Barry Schwartz, professor of psychology and economics at Swarthmore College and author of *Practical Wisdom*

"From Vietnam to Iraq, Sony to ICI, chess to mountaineering, John Kay tells a fast-paced detective story as he searches for the surprising secret to success in politics, business, and life. Kay is persuasive, rigorous, creative, and wise. Brilliant."

— Tim Harford, author of *The Undercover Economist* and *The Logic of Life*

"John Kay builds on a great philosophical tradition—stretching back through Charles Darwin and Adam Smith—that understands how remarkable things can be achieved without anybody understanding how or even intending them. He has taken this idea and applied it with style to modern conundrums from the physics behind Beckham's goals to the mathematics behind Buffett's riches. A great book."

— Matt Ridley, author of *Genome* and *Nature Via Nurture*

"An ingenious riff about unintended consequences."

— Stephen Bayley, architecture and design and critic for *The Observer* and author of *A Dictionary of Idiocy*, *Cars*, and *Design*

"A very timely and clever book."

— Anthony Seldon, author of *Blair*, *Blair Unbound*, and *Trust*

PENGUIN BOOKS

OBLIQUITY

John Kay is a visiting professor at the London School of Economics and a fellow of St John's College, University of Oxford. As research director and director, he established the Institute for Fiscal Studies as one of Britain's most respected think tanks. Since then he has been a professor at the London Business School and the University of Oxford, where he was the first director of the Saïd Business School. He is a regular columnist for the Financial Times. For more information, visit www.johnkay.com.

Obliquity

WHY OUR GOALS ARE BEST ACHIEVED INDIRECTLY

JOHN KAY

PENGUIN BOOKS

PENGUIN BOOKS

Published by the Penguin Group

Penguin Group (USA) Inc., 375 Hudson Street, New York, New York 10014, U.S.A. · Penguin Group
(Canada), 90 Eglinton Avenue East, Suite 700, Toronto, Ontario, Canada M4P 2Y3 (a division of
Pearson Penguin Canada Inc.) · Penguin Books Ltd, 80 Strand, London WC2R 0RL, England ·
Penguin Ireland, 25 St. Stephen's Green, Dublin 2, Ireland (a division of Penguin Books Ltd) ·
Penguin Books Australia Ltd, 250 Camberwell Road, Camberwell, Victoria 3124, Australia
(a division of Pearson Australia Group Pty Ltd) · Penguin Books India Pvt Ltd, 11 Community
Centre, Panchsheel Park, New Delhi – 110 017, India · Penguin Group (NZ), 67 Apollo Drive,
Rosedale, Auckland 0632, New Zealand (a division of Pearson New Zealand Ltd) · Penguin Books
(South Africa) (Pty) Ltd, 24 Sturdee Avenue, Rosebank, Johannesburg 2196, South Africa

Penguin Books Ltd, Registered Offices: 80 Strand, London WC2R 0RL, England

First published in Great Britain by Profile Books 2010
First published in the United States of America by The Penguin Press,
a member of Penguin Group (USA) Inc. 2011
Published in Penguin Books 2012

Copyright © John Kay, 2010
All rights reserved

Illustration credits:
Pages 7, 58, 112, 113 (The Watson Test, part 1): Sue Lamble
9 (top): Roger Viollet / Getty Images
9 (bottom): Getty Images
56 (top): Superstock
56 (bottom): Private collection / James Goodman Gallery, New York, USA / Bridgeman
95: From Blastland and Dilnot
113 (photographs, left to right): Bob Barkany; Juan Silva; DAJ; Image Source
117: ML Design

THE LIBRARY OF CONGRESS HAS CATALOGED THE HARDCOVER EDITION AS FOLLOWS:
Kay, J. A. (John Anderson)
Obliquity : why our goals are best achieved indirectly / by John Kay.
p.   cm.
Includes bibliographical references and index.
ISBN 978 1 59420 278 0 (hc.)
ISBN 978 0 14 312055 1 (pb.)
1. Success.   2. Goal (Psychology)   I. Title.
BF637.S8K39   2011
155.8   dc22
2010050269

DESIGNED BY AMANDA DEWEY

Except in the United States of America, this book is sold subject to the condition that it shall not, by
way of trade or otherwise, be lent, resold, hired out, or otherwise circulated without the publisher's
prior consent in any form of binding or cover other than that in which it is published and without
a similar condition including this condition being imposed on the subsequent purchaser.

The scanning, uploading, and distribution of this book via the Internet or via any other means
without the permission of the publisher is illegal and punishable by law. Please purchase only
authorized electronic editions and do not participate in or encourage electronic piracy
of copyrightable materials. Your support of the author's rights is appreciated.

ALWAYS LEARNING   PEARSON

CONTENTS

PART ONE
. . . .

The Oblique World:
How Obliquity Surrounds Us

PART TWO
....

The Need for Obliquity:
Why We Often Can't Solve Problems Directly

CONCLUSIONS

Obliquity

PREFACE

For over ten years, I built and ran an economic consultancy business, and much of our revenue was derived from selling models to large corporate clients. One day I asked myself a question: If these models were helpful, why did we not build similar models for our own decision making? The answer, I realized, was that our customers didn't really use these models for their decision making either. They used them internally or externally to justify decisions that they had already made.

They were playing what I now call Franklin's gambit, after Benjamin Franklin. He wrote: "So convenient a thing is it to be a reasonable creature, since it enables one to find or make a reason for everything one had a mind to do."[1] Franklin's remark about hindsight rationalization is particularly significant, not just because he was a clever man but because, as I will describe in chapter ten, he has come to be regarded as the founding father of scientific decision making.

Of course, we told ourselves privately, our clients were

being stupid—that was why they didn't use our models. But we didn't think *we* were stupid, and we didn't use them either. I can remember a couple of occasions on which a spreadsheet analysis did help us to solve problems of our own, both of them related to the financing of the business. But that was all.

Like many economists we believed that if our models did not describe the world, the fault lay with the world, not the model. But it isn't just economists who make that mistake. Politicians, investors and bankers, businesspeople believe that although they don't solve problems according to a standard model of rational decision making, they ought to. So they pretend that they do—to others, and perhaps to themselves.

We prefer to tell stories than to use analytic models, and the best and most helpful models are, at their root, narratives. This book presents its messages through stories because, as every teacher or consultant knows, that is the method through which we best absorb arguments and make sense of a complex world. But stories can mislead as well as inform; we must build our stories from the evidence—not, as in Franklin's gambit, build our evidence to match narratives we have previously constructed.

It is more than a decade since I escaped from an activity of which I was increasingly skeptical. Since then, I have seen disasters perpetrated by people who played Franklin's gambit in both politics and business, in Iraq and on Wall Street. Mistakes made by those who could find a reason for everything they had a mind to do, and did: who tried to make the world conform to their view of the world.

These failures of both policy and prediction have encouraged economists and other social scientists to look at what people actually do rather than imposing on them models of how economists think people should behave. One popular book with this approach adopts the title *Predictably Irrational*.[2] But this title reflects the same mistake that my colleagues and I made when we privately disparaged our clients for their stupidity. If people are predictably irrational, perhaps they are not irrational at all: Perhaps the fault lies not with the world but with our concept of rationality. Perhaps we should think differently about how we really make decisions and solve problems. Perhaps we should recognize the ubiquity, and inevitability, of obliquity.

The term *obliquity* was suggested to me by Sir James Black, the Nobel Prize–winning pharmacologist whose contribution to the development of ICI's pharmaceutical business is described in chapter three. In the course of verifying that history, I talked to Black about his reasons for leaving ICI to join another British pharmaceutical company, SmithKline. At SmithKline Black discovered another blockbuster drug, and the indirect effect was to stimulate a third company, Glaxo, to create and market Zantac, which would become the world's best-selling prescription drug.

Black probably created more shareholder value than any other man in postwar British business, but his motivation was to pursue chemistry, not profit. He left ICI, he told me, because his interests were in furthering his research, not helping to market his discoveries. "I used to tell my colleagues [at ICI] that if they wanted profits, there were many easier routes than drug research. How wrong could I have been!" he told me, and went on,

"I call it the principle of obliquity: Goals are often best achieved without intending them."

Black died two days before the first, British, edition of this book was published. I hope it is not presumptuous to dedicate this American edition to a British scientist whose modesty was as remarkable as his talent.

Chapter 1

OBLIQUITY—
Why Our Objectives Are Often
Best Pursued Indirectly

I never, indeed, wavered in the conviction that happiness is the test
of all rules of conduct, and the end of life. But I now thought that
this end was only to be attained by not making it the direct end.
Those only are happy (I thought) who have their minds fixed on
some object other than their own happiness; on the happiness of
others, on the improvement of mankind, even on some art or
pursuit, followed not as a means, but as itself an ideal end. Aiming
thus at something else, they find happiness by the way.

—John Stuart Mill, *Autobiography*[1]

Visionary companies pursue a cluster of objectives, of which making
money is only one—and not necessarily the primary one. Yes, they
seek profits, but they're equally guided by a core ideology—core
values and sense of purpose beyond just making money. Yet
paradoxically, the visionary companies make more money than the
purely profit driven companies.

—Jim Collins and Jerry I. Porras, *Built to Last*[2]

He is in this, as in many other cases, led by an invisible hand to promote an end which was no part of his intention. By pursuing his own interest he frequently promotes that of society more effectually than when he really intends to promote it.

—Adam Smith, *The Wealth of Nations*[3]

Tell all the truth, but tell it slant. Success in circuit lies.

—Emily Dickinson[4]

The American continent separates the Atlantic Ocean in the east from the Pacific in the west. The route of the Panama Canal follows the shortest crossing of America. When you arrive at Balboa port on the Pacific coast you are some thirty miles to the east of Colón, where you left the Atlantic. The best route follows a southeasterly direction. The shortest straight line running from east to west goes through Nicaragua, and this "direct" route is much longer.

The people who first found this route weren't looking west, and they weren't looking for oceans. Keats attributed the find to

stout Cortez when with eagle eyes
He star'd at the Pacific—and all his men
Look'd at each other with a wild surmise—
Silent, upon a peak in Darien.[5]

Balboa, not Cortés, was actually the first European to see the Pacific, but Keats had the right general idea. The way to the

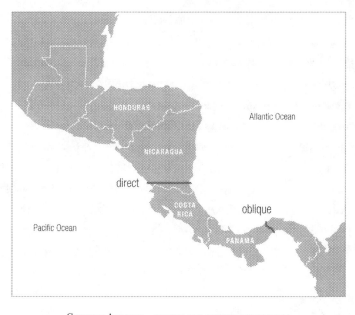

CENTRAL AMERICA—DIRECT AND OBLIQUE CROSSINGS
Sue Lamble

ocean was found by conquistadores who sought silver and gold, not oceans. Not only was the route oblique, but so was the means of its discovery.

The problem of finding the best traverse of America is easier than most problems we face in business, politics or our personal lives. We have almost complete knowledge of the territory and it doesn't change—or doesn't change much: The warming of the Arctic seas may make the Northwest Passage a navigable route, enabling ships to sail routinely from Atlantic to Pacific without using a canal at all. In the meantime, however, the best route will remain the Panama Canal. Ships go eastward in order to reach their western destinations more quickly and economically. They follow a trajectory that is oblique. *Obliquity* describes the process of achieving complex objectives indirectly.

In general, oblique approaches recognize that complex objectives tend to be imprecisely defined and contain many elements that are not necessarily or obviously compatible with one another, and that we learn about the nature of the objectives and the means of achieving them during a process of experiment and discovery. Oblique approaches often step backward to move forward. All these things were true of the activities that engaged Cortés (or Balboa). Like other great achievers, they tackled problems whose nature emerged only as they solved them.

In the twentieth century, technology emancipated builders from tradition and accumulated knowledge. Some architects believed that they could dispense with the oblique approach, the practice of incremental modification of concepts and observances enshrined in long-accepted conventions. They preferred deduction from first principles and believed that the direct could replace the oblique. There were many straight lines in their drawings.

The hope that rational design by an omniscient planner could supersede practical knowledge derived from a process of adaptation and discovery swept across many fields in the course of the twentieth century. This approach was generally described as modernism.[6]

The architectural commentator Charles Jencks declared that modernism ended at 3:32 P.M. on July 15, 1972, when demolition contractors detonated fuses to blow up the Pruitt-Igoe housing project in St. Louis.[7] Less than two decades earlier, the scheme had won awards for its pioneering, visionary architec-

Le Corbusier's Unité d'habitation, Marseille
Roger Viollet/Getty Images

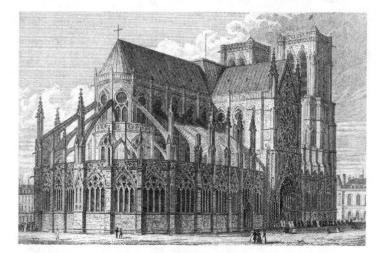

Notre Dame, Paris
Getty Images

ture. Tower blocks were the supreme expression of le Corbusier's view that "a house is a machine for living in."[8] Le Corbusier himself designed the first such buildings in Marseille.[9] The Unités d'Habitation were the product of one man's vision and were planned in detail—down to the furnishing of the flats—right from the start.

The modernists knew less than they thought. A house is not simply a machine for living in, as Le Corbusier had declared it to be. There is a difference between a house and a home. The functions of a home are complex: The utility of a building depends not only on its design but also on the reactions of those who live in it. The occupants of the Pruitt-Igoe project were alienated by an environment that saw no need for oblique, unplanned social interactions. They disliked the projects, they hated their apartments, they trashed the common areas. The practicality of the buildings proved, in the end, not to be practical.

An oblique approach recognizes that what we want from a home, or a community, has many elements. We will never succeed in specifying fully what they are, and to the extent that we do, we discover that they are often incompatible and inconsistent. The interactions between a home and its occupants, or among the people who make up a community, are complex and uncertain. Experience of both previous and current problems guides the search for answers. Many people contribute to the outcome, and even after that outcome has been realized none of them necessarily holds a full understanding of how it came about. That is how the cathedral of Notre Dame was built, by many hands over several centuries.

Reengineering the Corporation, by Michael Hammer and James Champy, was one of the best-selling business books of the 1990s, and Hammer and Champy were as radical in aspiration as Le Corbusier:

> These ideas, we believe, are as important to business today as Adam Smith's ideas were to the entrepreneurs and managers of the last two centuries. [Reengineering] means asking the question "If I were re-creating this company today, given what I know and given current technology, what would it look like?" Reengineering a company means tossing aside old systems and starting over. It involves going back to the beginning and inventing a better way of doing work.[10]

Reengineering was the substitution of design for adaptation and discovery—preferring the direct to the oblique.

The demand for such a direct approach found a manifesto in Lenin's *What Is to Be Done?*[11] The future Russian leader argued that political and economic reform could be achieved only if imposed by a close-knit revolutionary cadre with a single vision. And although Le Corbusier was as far to the right as Lenin was to the left, and Hammer and Champy were certainly no Marxists, Le Corbusier would have approved wholeheartedly. Reengineering was the essence of his conception.

> It has been drawn up by serene and lucid minds. It has taken account of nothing but human truths. It has ignored all current regulations, all existing usages and channels.[12]

I cannot read such words without thinking of Pol Pot, who proclaimed that the Khmer Rouge takeover of Cambodia marked year zero, when everything began anew (two centuries earlier, the French revolutionaries made the same claim). A reign of terror followed in both cases. Pol Pot not only destroyed the fabric of society but also killed or caused the deaths of some 1.5 million of his countrymen.

Hammer and Champy are not bad men. Perhaps they do not really mean what they appear to say, and reengineering should be seen as a thought experiment, a way of asking questions about the relevance of current practice, not a literal prescription. Still, Lenin and Le Corbusier did mean what they said. What they believed to be the height of rationality, the creation of "serene and lucid minds," was not rational at all, because it was based on a false and oversimplified picture of the world. The environment—social, commercial, natural—in which we operate changes over time and as we interact with it. Our knowledge of that complex environment is necessarily piecemeal and imperfect. And so objectives are generally best accomplished obliquely rather than directly.

This book is divided into three parts. In part one (chapters two through six) I will illustrate the role of obliquity in our personal and our working lives. Happiness is not achieved through the pursuit of happiness. The most profitable businesses are not the most profit oriented. The wealthiest people are not those most assertive in the pursuit of wealth. The greatest paintings are not the most accurate representations of their subjects; the forests most resistant to fires are not the ones whose foresters are best at putting out fires. Soviet planners managed the economy far less successfully than the adaptive, disorganized processes of market economies.

In part two (chapters seven through twelve) I will describe the factors that make direct approaches impracticable for so many problems and demonstrate the need for obliquity. Our objectives are often necessarily loosely described and frequently have elements that are not just incompatible but incapable of being compared with one another. The consequences of our actions depend on the responses of other people, and these responses spring not just from our actions but from their perceptions of our motives for undertaking these actions. We deal with complex systems whose structure we can understand only imperfectly. The problems we face are rarely completely specified, and the environment in which we tackle them contains irresolvable uncertainties.

In part three (chapters thirteen through twenty) I describe the oblique approach to problem solving and decision making. In obliquity there are no predictable connections between intentions and outcomes. Oblique problem solvers do not evaluate all available alternatives: they make successive choices from a narrow range of options. Effective decision makers are distinguished not so much by the superior extent of their knowledge as by their being aware of its limitations. Problem solving is iterative and adaptive rather than direct. Good decision makers are not identified by their ability to provide compelling accounts of how they reached their conclusions. The most complex systems come into being, and function, without anyone having knowledge of the whole. Good decision makers are eclectic and

tend to regard consistency as a mark of stubbornness, or ideo-
logical blindness, rather than as a virtue. Rationality is not defined by good processes; irrationality lies in persisting with
methods and actions that plainly do not work—including the
methods and actions that commonly masquerade as rationality.

PART ONE

The Oblique World: How Obliquity Surrounds Us

Chapter 2

FULFILLMENT—
How the Happiest People
Do Not Pursue Happiness

In 1980 Reinhold Messner performed perhaps the most spectacular mountaineering feat ever accomplished. He reached the summit of Everest from the more difficult Tibetan side alone and without oxygen. "I can scarcely go on. . . . No despair, no happiness, no anxiety," he wrote. "I have not lost the mastery of my feelings, there are actually no more feelings. I consist only of will."[1]

Messner was trying to achieve many things—to see the world from its highest point, to complete a demanding climb, to achieve fame and personal satisfaction. He sought happiness by enduring misery, he chose the most demanding route, he deprived himself of aids that would have made his progress safer and his success more probable. He achieved his objective obliquely by overcoming obstacles he had placed in his own path.

Climbing high mountains is dangerous and exhausting. The people who undertake it face freezing cold; they fight for breath and are prone to sickness. Asked why they do it, they frequently repeat the unsatisfactory answer attributed to George Mallory, who died on Everest in 1924 and may have been the first man to reach the summit: "Because it is there."[2] When pressed, they elaborate these answers with explanations that can be interpreted as a search for self-esteem, prestige or fulfillment.

Mountaineering is an extreme example of an apparently unpleasant activity undertaken by people who could be comfortable but choose not to be. There are many other such activities. These routes to happiness are oblique. We chase a ball around a field until we are too tired to stand. We make ourselves cold, wet and exhausted. We climb mountains only to descend again, we swim out to sea to be thrown back on land, we run until we cannot run any more. The determinants of happiness are evidently complicated.

The psychologist Mihalyi Csikszentmihalyi uses the term *flow* to describe the sensation people experience while engaged in demanding activities. It is "the sense of effortless action they feel [that] tends to occur when a person's skills are fully involved in overcoming a challenge that is just about manageable."[3] Flow is often achieved at work. The experiences I associate with flow are lectures or seminars that seem to be going really well, the silence of an audience that is hanging on the next word or the sensation of writing when, as occasionally happens, the words seem, well, to flow. But many flow experiences come in leisure activities, such as surfing or ball games, or in other recreation, such as making music or fashioning sculptures: activities whose only purpose is the activity itself.

People experiencing flow do not say they are happy: Csikszentmihalyi asks his subjects to report regularly on their state of mind, and they are more likely to tell him they are happy when they are socializing with friends than when they are in flow. Perhaps people in flow are just too busy to be happy. But flow experiences seem to contribute greatly to long-term well-being. That is presumably why Mallory went back to the mountains until he died.

Csikszentmihalyi reports that many people describe their flow experiences as "moments that stand out as being the best in their lives." If he is right—and most readers will recognize the feelings he describes—then the people who seek happiness in these oblique and superficially unpromising ways are not making mistakes. Through experiences we normally associate with unhappiness they achieve greater happiness than if they had sought happiness directly.

Perhaps people are confused about what makes them happy.[4] Anyone who has changed a diaper, or failed to quiet a childish tantrum, will recognize that looking after children is an oblique route to happiness. Csikszentmihalyi reports that people are happier when they are at work than when they're caring for a child, and researchers observe that reported happiness increases sharply when children leave home.[5] Yet many people also say that bringing up their children was the best experience of their life.

Perhaps, under social pressure to applaud the experience of child rearing, people say their children make them happy even though that is not how they really feel. But it's more likely that people who say that bringing up their children has made them very happy are telling the truth. And when the same people say that much of the time they spent with their children was not happy, they are also telling the truth. Mountaineers like Messner do not say that being cold, starved of oxygen and at frequent risk of injury or death makes them happy. They confirm the commonsense assumption that such experiences are unpleasant. But the experience of having accomplished a difficult climb makes them immensely happy. They are not contradicting themselves, because happiness is not simply the aggregate of happy moments.

We have methods of creating happy, or at least happier, moments. Some people avoid depression by taking antidepressants or achieve pleasurable experiences through drugs. This way of life was satirized in Aldous Huxley's *Brave New World*.[6] Education was directed at making people believe they were happy and a drug, soma, removed any residual negative feelings. As we learn more about the chemical processes in the brain that are associated with states we describe as happy or unhappy, the idea of Huxley's drug is no longer science fiction. There could be a very direct route to happiness.

But are those who seek happiness in this way really happy? The philosopher Robert Nozick imagined an experience machine that would not only enable the user to create any desired sensation but also make it possible to forget that he or she was linked to the machine.[7] But, he suggested, we might not want to use it. Nozick thought not only that oblique approaches were the best route to happiness but also that they were the only route to real happiness. He also thought most people would agree with him. The belief that there is an underlying notion of real happiness that is distinct from feelings of happiness seems to be one that is widely shared.

Oscar Wilde's Dorian Gray sought the directness of the experience machine: "A man who is master of himself can end a sorrow as he can invent an emotion. I don't want to be at the mercy of my emotions. I want to use them, to enjoy them and to dominate them."[8] Wilde's *The Picture of Dorian Gray* is one exploration of the Faustian theme, in which the soul is traded for transitory pleasures. The enduring popularity of this motif is an expression of our knowledge that we often sacrifice our real objective by pursuing what we want.

Happiness is not achieved through the frequent repetition of favorable experiences, and that is why *the pursuit of happiness* is a peculiar phrase. It is easy to see why the Founding Fathers chose that language to describe their aspirations. While the potential citizens of the United States might assert the right to life and to liberty, to claim a right to happiness would be presumptuous. But happiness is not best achieved by its pursuit, and those who pursue happiness misunderstand its nature.

The difficulties of pursuing happiness begin with the difficulty of knowing what it is we pursue. A heartwarming film, *The Pursuit of Happyness* (sic)[9] stars Will Smith in a rags-to-riches story. Loosely based on an account by Chris Gardner,[10] it tells of an African American kid who rises from homelessness through the brokerage firms Dean Witter and Bear Stearns to become chief executive of a securities trading business. For Gardner, the pursuit of happiness begins when he sees a broker in a red Ferrari in a hospital parking lot. From then on, drive and ambition take him directly to the top. Eventually Gardner himself acquires a red Ferrari.

But this story tells us more about modern American life and values than about happiness. Happiness is not a red Ferrari. In advanced countries, the proportion of people who say they are happy has remained broadly constant over time as incomes have increased. Countries such as Nigeria, where poverty is widespread by any standard, have average levels of reported happiness comparable to those of the United States or Western Europe. Although average happiness does not necessarily rise with average income, higher-income households consistently report greater happiness than poorer households—that is the lure of the red Ferrari.

The achievement of happiness is a matter of personal fulfillment rather than objective circumstances. People with severe disabilities, such as paraplegics, mostly describe themselves as happy. They are much happier than people believe they would be if they were themselves to suffer from paraplegia. The capacity of humans to survive appalling circumstances, and emerge little affected, is an extraordinary testimony to our powers of adaptation.[11]

Happiness is where you find it, not where you look for it. The shortest crossing of America was found by seekers for gold, not explorers of oceans. The discovery of happiness, like the discovery of new territory, is usually oblique.

Chapter 3

THE PROFIT-SEEKING PARADOX—
How the Most Profitable Companies
Are Not the Most Profit Oriented

For most of the twentieth century, ICI was Britain's largest and most successful manufacturing company. In 1990 ICI described its business purpose:

> ICI aims to be the world's leading chemical company, serving customers internationally through the innovative and responsible application of chemistry and related science.
>
> Through achievement of our aim, we will enhance the wealth and well-being of our shareholders, our employees, our customers and the communities which we serve and in which we operate.[1]

ICI's business had evolved over the decades through changing interpretations of the "responsible application of chemistry." The company had translated its traditional strengths in dyestuffs and explosives into new chemical businesses—petrochemicals and agricultural fertilizers and finally, after the Second World War, pharmaceuticals.

But this strategic decision was slow to bring returns. The pharmaceutical division was a continuing drain on ICI resources until the discovery of beta-blockers in the 1960s gave the company the first effective drug for controlling hypertension. More discoveries followed, and in the next two decades pharmaceuticals became the growth engine of ICI.

The research capabilities developed in ICI provided a pool of talent from which other companies, like Glaxo and SmithKline French, found ideas and people. In particular, SmithKline recruited James Black, the chemist behind beta-blockers, who was frustrated that ICI was emphasizing profit over science. Black went on to discover a new group of blockbusting drugs, antiulcerants. These transformed the profitability of first SmithKline and then Glaxo, whose innovative product Zantac was a runaway success. ICI's decision to enter pharmaceuticals ultimately led to the development of a British global pharmaceutical industry, perhaps the greatest achievement in postwar British business.

In 1991, a predatory takeover specialist, Hanson Trust, bought a modest stake in ICI. While the threat to the company's independence did not last long, the effects on the approach adopted by the company's senior executives were galvanizing. Directness was the order of the day. The company restructured its operations and floated the pharmaceutical division as a separate business, Zeneca. The rump business of ICI declared a new mission statement: "The ICI Group's vision is to be the industry leader in creating value for customers and shareholders through market leadership, technological edge and a world competitive cost base."[2]

The company embarked on an extensive program of acquisitions and disposals that failed in every respect, including that of creating shareholder value. The share price peaked in 1997, a few months after the new strategy was announced. The decline thereafter was relentless. In 2007, ICI ceased to exist as an independent company. The responsible application of chemistry not only created a better business than did the attempts at creating value: It also created more value.

When I taught strategy at London Business School in the early 1990s, I told students that Boeing's grip on the world civil aviation market made it the most powerful market leader in world business. Just as ICI was committed to chemistry, so Boeing was committed to airplanes. Bill Allen was chief executive from 1945 to 1968. Under Allen, the corporate purpose was to "eat, breathe, and sleep the world of aeronautics."[3]

During Allen's tenure Boeing developed the 737. With almost four thousand planes in the air, it is the most successful passenger airliner in history. But the company's largest and riskiest project was the development of the 747 jumbo jet. When a nonexecutive director asked for details of the expected return on investment, he was brushed off: Some studies had been made, he was told, but the manager concerned couldn't remember the result.[4] By the early 1990s Boeing had established almost complete dominance of world civil aviation. Boeing created the most commercially successful aircraft company, not through love of profit but through love of planes. The oblique approach to profitability delivered spectacular results.

Yet it took only ten years for Boeing to prove me wrong in asserting that its market position in civil aviation was impregnable. A decisive shift in corporate culture followed the acquisition of the company's chief U.S. rival, McDonnell Douglas. The new CEO, Phil Condit, explained that the company's previous preoccupation with meeting "technological challenges of supreme magnitude" would have to change.[5] Directness would displace obliquity: "We are going into a value based environment where unit cost, return on investment, shareholder return are the measures by which you'll be judged. That's a big shift."[6] The company put the location of its corporate headquarters up for auction, and its senior executives agreed to move from Seattle, where the main production facilities were located, to Chicago. The newly focused business reviewed risky investments in new civil projects with much greater skepticism and made a strategic decision to redirect resources toward projects for the U.S. military that involved low financial risk. Chicago had the advantage of being nearer to Washington, where government funds were dispensed.

So Boeing's civil order book fell behind that of Airbus, the European consortium. The aims of Airbus were not initially commercial but, by oblique chance, Europe's champion became a profitable business. Boeing's strategy of getting close to the Pentagon proved counterproductive: The company got rather too close and faced allegations of corruption.[7] And what was the market's verdict on the company's performance in terms of unit cost, return on investment and shareholder return? Boeing stock, thirty-two dollars when Condit took over, rose to fifty-nine dollars as he affirmed the commitment to shareholder value; by the time of his forced resignation in December 2003 it had fallen to thirty-four dollars.

Condit's successors once again emphasized civil aviation. The 777 is a success, and the Dreamliner appears a better vehicle for the future than the huge Airbus 380. By 2008 Boeing had regained its leading position in commercial aviation and the share price its earlier value. At Boeing, as at ICI, shareholder value was most effectively created when sought obliquely.

That profit-seeking paradox, like the conundrum of happiness, illustrates the power of obliquity. Comparisons of the same companies over time are echoed in contrasts between different companies in the same industries. Jim Collins and Jerry Porras undertook paired comparisons between outstanding ("visionary") companies and adequate but less remarkable firms with similar operations. Merck and Pfizer was one such comparison. Collins and Porras compare the oblique philosophy of George Merck ("We try never to forget that medicine is for the people. It is not for the profits. The profits follow, and if we have remembered that, they have never failed to appear. The better we have remembered it, the larger they have been."[8]) with the directness of John McKeen of Pfizer ("So far as humanly possible, we aim to get profit out of everything we do."[9]).

Collins's book was published in 1994. Fifteen years later, in *How the Mighty Fall*, Collins would revisit the Merck story: "In his 1995 annual letter to shareholders, Merck's chairman and CEO, Ray Gilmartin, delineated the company's number one business objective: 'being a top-tier growth company.' The opening line of the chairman's letter in the 2000 annual report stated directly: "As a company, Merck is totally focussed on growth."[10]

Merck's shift to a more direct approach did not have a happy outcome. Both Merck and Pfizer would, in the late 1990s, bring to market a new class of drugs called COX-2 inhibitors. These products are powerful analgesics, and for some patients, who have difficulty in tolerating established anti-inflammatory drugs such as aspirin, COX-2 inhibitors have proved invaluable. But the best route to revenue growth was to promote these drugs to a mass market for which inexpensive substitutes were equally satisfactory.

Vioxx, Merck's product, aggravated heart conditions in a small minority of these patients. The company was slow to respond to reports of adverse reactions, but finally it withdrew Vioxx from the market and faced the prospect of extensive litigation from alleged victims of its promotional campaigns. Merck fell off *Fortune*'s list of most admired companies, on which it had occupied a prominent position for many years.[11]

Today the pharmaceutical company that has created the most value for its shareholders is Johnson & Johnson, whose oblique "credo" was first set out in 1943 by Robert Johnson, a scion of the founding family and company chairman for thirty years. "We believe our first responsibility is to the doctors, nurses and patients, to mothers and fathers and all others who use our products and services," the credo begins. It ends, many lines later, "When we operate according to these principles, the stockholders should realize a fair return."[12] Events seem to have proved Robert Johnson right.

Few companies go as far as Sony's declaration of its oblique approach to profit in its founding statement: "We shall eliminate any undue profit-seeking."[13] But Collins and Porras paired Hewlett-Packard with Texas Instruments, Procter & Gamble with Colgate, Marriott with Howard Johnson, and found the same result in each case: The company that put more emphasis on profit in its declaration of objectives was the less profitable in its financial statements.

There are many similar examples of the triumph of the oblique over the direct. Citigroup was created in 1998 as a result of the merger of Citicorp, the world's largest retail bank, with the Travelers financial group created by the ambitious Sandy Weill. The group structure featured Weill and the more cerebral John Reed of Citicorp as joint CEOs. Tension between the two men was evident from the beginning, not least in their vision of the business: "'The model I have is of a global consumer company that really helps the middle class with something they haven't been served well by historically,' [said Reed]. 'That's my vision. That's my dream.' 'My goal is increasing shareholder value,' Sandy [Weill] interjected, glancing frequently at a nearby computer monitor displaying Citigroup's changing stock price."[14]

Within a short time, Weill had displaced Reed. Then revelations of a range of improprieties at Citigroup tumbled out. By 2002 a shaken Weill would be asserting that "we must be conscious of a broader purpose than simply delivering profits."[15] Soon after, Weill himself was out of office, replaced by the lawyer Chuck Prince, with a brief to restore Citigroup's reputation.

But allegations of wrongdoing kept coming, to be followed by business disasters. As the credit expansion reached its apogee in 2007, Prince would tell the *Financial Times*: "So long as the music is playing, you have to get up and dance. We're still dancing."[16] But a month later, the music stopped. Prince would also soon lose his job, and by 2008 Citigroup would be surviving only on life support from the U.S. taxpayer. The merger had in less than a decade destroyed almost all the shareholder value in Citicorp.

The modern philosopher Alasdair MacIntyre contrasts the business of fishing—designed and planned—with the practice of fishing—the methods and traditions that have evolved over the generations in a fishing community. In the fishing business

> a fishing crew may be organised and understood as a purely technical and economic means to a productive end, whose aim is only or overridingly to satisfy as profitably as possible some market's demand for fish. . . . Not only the skills, but also the qualities of character valued by those who manage the organisation, will be those well designed to achieve a high level of profitability. And each individual at work as a member of such a fishing crew will value those qualities of character in her or himself or in others which are apt to produce a high level of reward for her or himself.

That is the sort of crew in which Sandy Weill would be comfortable, at least so long as he was captain. But MacIntyre admires the practice of fishing.

> Consider by contrast a crew whose members may well have initially joined for the sake of their wage or other share of

the catch, but who have acquired from the rest of the crew an understanding of and devotion to excellence in fishing and to excellence in playing one's part as a member of such a crew. . . . So the interdependence of the members of a fishing crew in respect of skills, the achievement of goods and the acquisition of virtues will extend to an interdependence of the families of crew members and perhaps beyond them to the whole society of a fishing village.[17]

For MacIntyre it appears self-evident that the first crew will catch more fish. But is he right? Or are the complex objectives of a business organization—including a fishery—better achieved by an equivalently complex process of balancing incomparable and incommensurable underlying values and goals? As so often, we have a Harvard Business School case to help us.[18] The Prelude Corporation, once the largest lobster producer in North America, sought to bring the techniques of modern management to the fishing industry. Listen to its president, Joseph S. Gaziano:

The fishing industry now is just like the automobile industry was 60 years ago: 100 companies are going to come and go, but we'll be the General Motors. . . . The technology and money required to fish offshore are so great that the little guy can't make out.

Soon after the case was written the Prelude Corporation exited the fishing business. It did so, moreover, for entirely explicable reasons—which emerge from MacIntyre's account. Lobster are still caught most effectively from small boats whose skippers hunt rather than manufacture their product. Success depends on the flair, skills and initiative of people who cannot be effectively supervised. The product of people who feel genuine commitment, who "have acquired from the rest of the crew an understanding of and devotion to excellence in fishing" exceeds that achieved when the "only aim is overridingly to satisfy as profitably as possible some market's desire for fish."[19] That is why MacIntyre's second crew is still fishing while his first is not.

George Merck and Robert Johnson created great businesses that, in consequence, made remarkable amounts of money for their shareholders. ICI and Boeing were more successful as profit-making companies when they "served customers internationally through the responsible application of chemistry" or "ate, breathed and slept the world of aeronautics" than when they tried to "maximise value for our shareholders" or "go into a value based environment."

But the last word in this chapter should go to Jack Welch, CEO of General Electric from 1981 to 2001. Welch was not just America's most admired businessman but a darling of Wall Street. The rise in the market capitalization of GE during Welch's tenure represented the greatest creation of shareholder value ever. Ten years into retirement, he told the *Financial Times:* "Shareholder value is the dumbest idea in the world."[20] Elaborating his thought to *BusinessWeek* a few days later, he explained:

> The job of a leader and his or her team is to deliver to commitments in the short term while investing in the long term health of the business. . . . Employees will benefit from job

security and better rewards. Customers will benefit from better products or services. Communities will benefit because successful companies and their employees give back. And obviously shareholders will benefit because they can count on companies who will deliver on both their short term commitments and long term vision.[21]

The route to profit was an oblique one.

Chapter 4

THE ART OF THE DEAL—
How the Wealthiest People
Are Not the Most Materialistic

Seventy years after his death, it is still hard to disentangle the mixture of motives that made John D. Rockefeller not only the world's richest man, but also its greatest philanthropist.

> I believe the power to make money is a gift from God—just as are the instincts for art, music, literature, the doctor's talent, the nurse's, yours—to be developed and used to the best of our ability for the good of mankind. Having been endowed with the gift I possess, I believe it is my duty to make money and still more money; and to use the money I make for the good of my fellow man according to the dictation of my conscience.[1]

Andrew Carnegie, the Scottish-born steel magnate and contemporary of Rockefeller, applied the same determination to giving his fortune away that he applied to building it. "The man who dies rich thus dies disgraced," he famously remarked.[2]

Henry Ford built the eponymous motor company because he was passionate about cars and passionate about bringing cars to a mass market. Once he was sued by a group of stockholders who demanded the corporation pay out larger dividends. The stockholders won the case. Most of the dividend went to Ford himself, who used the cash to buy back the minority interest. With hindsight, of course, the disgruntled shareholders would have done better to keep quiet.

Sam Walton, founder and principal shareholder of the world's largest retailer, would drive himself around in a pickup truck until his death. He recalled:

> I have concentrated all along on building the finest retailing company that we possibly could. Period. Creating a huge personal fortune was never particularly a goal of mine.[3]

But he did create a huge personal fortune: Four of the top twenty places in *Forbes*'s rich list are still occupied by members of the Walton family. I cannot honestly recommend that you read Bill Gates's accounts of his career, but if you do you will be left with a clear sense that the man's primary interest is in computers rather than cash, in building businesses rather than building monuments. Like Carnegie and Rockefeller, Gates has become a substantial philanthropist and has thrown himself with enthusiasm into the application of business methods to charitable purposes.

Even the egregious Donald Trump begins his autobiography, *The Art of the Deal*, with: "I don't do it for the money. I've got enough, much more money than I'll ever need. I do it to do it. Deals are my art form."[4] No doubt unconsciously, Trump echoes John Stuart Mill: He engages in "some art or pursuit, followed not as a means, but as itself an ideal end."[5]

Building a large and successful business, as did Rockefeller and Carnegie, Walton and Gates, requires exceptional talent and hard work, a devotion to business and to the detail of business. There is no reason to think these characteristics are linked to greed and materialism, rather the opposite. People who are obsessively interested in money are drawn to get-rich-quick schemes, legal or criminal, rather than business opportunities. When these schemes come off, as occasionally they do, they are inclined to retire to villas in the sun.

Even if we suspect an element of humbug in Rockefeller's assertion that making money is a gift from God, and find something ridiculous in Trump's claim that "deals are my art form," these statements tell us something about how these men approached the activities that made them rich. The richest men are not the most materialistic. Nor has it ever been otherwise.

Only in modern times has the principal route to great wealth been the development of a successful business. For most of history, and in much of the world today, the route to wealth was political and military power rather than business success. Yet the most successful acquirers of such wealth have been gripped by the quest for conquest and domination rather than material goals. We know little about Genghis Khan: Perhaps he would have told us that rape and pillage were his art form.

We know more about colonial conquerors. Many of the

Britons who looted India in the eighteenth century had motives that were primarily economic. But the most successful of these adventurers, Robert Clive, returned in 1760 to England, aged thirty-five. Ennobled as Lord Clive, he owned a fortune beyond imagination. He soon returned to India to establish the East India Company's administration in Bengal. Widely criticized for his part in the corruption that was endemic in that administration, he committed suicide in 1774.

Clive could have, while still a young man, enjoyed the wealth he had accumulated. He chose to return to a Bengal climate that sapped the health of most Englishmen who worked there. When his administration was criticized, he defended himself and then, finding the criticism unbearable, killed himself. However misguided we may now think it, Clive's colonial mission was not just a route to a fortune but an end in itself.

Personal exploitation on a large scale is today undertaken not by colonists but by local rulers: men such as Sani Abacha of Nigeria and Mobutu Sese Seko of Zaire, who looted billions from their countries' treasuries. Through most of their careers— perhaps even to the end of them—these men could have retired to a life of unhassled luxury. I write this overlooking Cap Martin, the idyllic peninsula on the French Riviera on which Mobutu owned four villas. But Abacha and Mobutu died in office. They preferred the joys of power to the fruits of larceny. Like Clive, their overriding objective was power, and their great wealth was a means of sustaining that power.

Those who most value the trappings of wealth are often those on whom it has been bestowed by chance. Richard Conniff, who has attempted an anthropological study of the very wealthy, provides a characteristic example:

> One night at a charity event in Palm Beach, I sat next to a woman in a hot pink Escada evening gown with black polka dots, her breasts served up like ripe fruit, her hair swept round in an ice cream whirl. She told me that she drove a new Jaguar, that she had places in Palm Beach, New York and the Hamptons, and that her gown had cost $4,000. A little later, after two or three glasses of wine, she confessed that her fortune had come from a rubber stamp business founded by her immigrant father. He was so frugal that he used to patch the torn seat of her office chair with Scotch tape rather than waste money replacing it. He kept the heat in his building so low that when his daughter did office work for him she had to wear a hat and gloves.[6]

For some, the accumulation of wealth is an end in itself. The richest woman of the American gilded age, Hetty Green, inherited a modest fortune from her father. Through successful investment she parlayed her assets into a large fortune. When her son suffered a knee infection, she unsuccessfully sought assistance from a charity hospital: The leg became gangrenous and was ultimately amputated. Green took no interest in material possessions and shuffled between small apartments to avoid tax.[7] She qualifies for an entry in the *Guinness World Records* as the world's greatest miser. She appears to have suffered from a pathological addiction to the accumulation of wealth for its own sake.

Green is an extreme case. Mobutu and Abacha certainly enjoyed the material benefits they assiduously collected. Nor did Rockefeller or Carnegie, Gates or Trump live Spartan existences. But others, like Sam Walton or the socialite's father, enjoyed the manifestations of wealth far less than much poorer men.

Warren Buffett today rivals Gates for the title of the world's richest man. Buffett enjoys his wealth as a demonstration of his skill as an investor, not for the material goods it brings. He still lives in the Omaha bungalow he bought almost fifty years ago and continues to take pleasure in a Nebraska steak washed down with Cherry Coke. After several years in which he described his corporate jet to his shareholders as "The Indefensible," he sold it and bought the largest shared-ownership aircraft business—the whole company.

Buffett's life and approach—and perhaps even more that of George Soros, another of today's legendary investors—was foretold by Aristotle's account of Thales of Miletus:

> People had been saying reproachfully to him that philosophy was useless, as it had left him a poor man. But he, deducing from his knowledge of the stars that there would be a good crop of olives, while it was still winter, and he had a little money to spare, used it to pay deposits on all the oil-presses in Miletus and Chios, thus securing their hire. This cost him only a small sum, as there were no other bidders. Then the time of the olive harvest came, and as there was a sudden and simultaneous demand for oil-presses he hired them out at any price he liked to ask. He made a lot of money and so demonstrated that it is easy for philosophers

to become rich, if they want to; but that is not their objective in life.[8]

I like that story and sometimes thought of it as I wondered
why senior executives insisted on paying themselves so much.
Why was it so important to receive money they did not need
and would never have time to spend? The remuneration was
necessary, I realized, to sustain their sense of their own importance. What self-respecting chief executive would accept that he
should be paid in the bottom quartile of CEO salaries in comparable companies—although, by definition, a quarter of people
must find themselves in that position? Even among City and Wall
Street traders and investment bankers, rightly identified as exemplars of greed, bonuses matter as much for the kudos they
confer as for the cash they generate. Why else would they be so
obsessed by the sums paid to their colleagues and competitors?

But the direct pursuit of wealth, whether as an end in itself or for the possessions it brings, tends to damage both the
individuals and organizations that seek it. Buffett is a rare ex-
ception, treating his success with engaging if slightly affected
self-deprecation and maintaining a commitment to strong ethical values. While the representation of the successful businessman as an aggressive bully is a popular caricature, that style
rarely makes for good business. Trump, the founding star of the
American television show *The Apprentice*, is a complex character
who revels in self-parody. His British counterpart, Alan Sugar,
appears to take himself more seriously.

The Apprentice encourages its participants to engage in
self-interested displays that in most contexts—including most

business contexts—are not only offensive but also counterproductive. The most garish publicist for this management style was Al Dunlap, who noisily proclaimed the cause of shareholder value through the 1990s, acquiring the nickname "Rambo in pinstripes." The cover of his book *Mean Business* features a picture of Rambo with two dogs. He describes his philosophy: "If you want a friend, get a dog. I'm taking no chances, I've got two."[9] There was no element of obliquity (or subtlety) for Rambo in pinstripes. Dunlap had no patience with any view of the corporation except as a machine to generate money for its stockholders and, most important, for Dunlap himself. In the end he was forced out of his post at Sunbeam, the appliance manufacturer, amid allegations of accounting abuse and profit manipulation. The corporation went bankrupt. Dunlap was spared possible civil and criminal suits only after he agreed to pay penalties and restitution of fifteen million dollars.[10]

The history of the last two decades is littered with fallen idols who, like Dunlap, stridently asserted the primacy of wealth. Gordon Gekko, the antihero of Oliver Stone's 1987 film *Wall Street*, famously proclaimed: "Greed is good." Gekko was partly based on Ivan Boesky, a notorious corporate raider of the 1980s, who was reported as telling a class at Columbia: "I want you to know that I think greed is healthy. You can be greedy and still feel good about yourself."[11] Soon after, Boesky went to prison, convicted of insider trading.

The businesses that epitomized the explosion of greed on Wall Street in the 1980s were Salomon Brothers (the firm mercilessly caricatured in Michael Lewis's *Liar's Poker*)[12] and Drexel

Burnham Lambert (more gently pilloried in Connie Bruck's *The Predators' Ball*).[13] Salomon turned bond trading from a backwater into the activity of choice for the financially ambitious, while Drexel Burnham Lambert pioneered the issue of junk bonds. Salomon, whose abuses had exhausted the patience of the U.S. Treasury, had to be rescued by Warren Buffett (in a rare error) and was eventually taken over by Citigroup (which closed its trading operations). Drexel Burnham Lambert collapsed.

In the following decade, the byword for greed was Bankers Trust, which sold derivative programs to large corporations and local authorities. Its reputation in tatters, the organization was acquired by Deutsche Bank. In the twenty-first century, the mantle of Salomon, Drexel and Bankers Trust was assumed by Bear Stearns and Lehman. Bear Stearns faced collapse in the spring of 2008 and was absorbed into JPMorgan Chase with substantial assistance from the U.S. taxpayer. Lehman famously went bankrupt in September 2008, its CEO, Dick Fuld, justifying his three-hundred-million-dollar remuneration to the end and beyond.[14]

In this chapter and the last, I've described the most spectacular exemplars of the era of corporate and financial-sector greed—Citigroup, Bear Stearns and Lehman, before them Salomon, Drexel and Bankers Trust. The common feature of every one of these companies is that huge sums of money were made by individuals in them but the business itself ultimately incurred massive losses of money, reputation or both. No deep knowledge of finance is needed to understand why these companies were financially successful only briefly and commercial failures in the long run. A corporate culture that extols greed cannot, in the end, protect itself against its own employees. Nor does the business with such a culture attract public sympathy when things go wrong (although large bailouts were provided to limit the damage their collapse imposed or would have imposed on the wider economy).

The motives that make for success in business are commitment to, passion for, business, which is not at all the same as love of money—a lesson that Lehman did not learn. "I think Lehman went under in part because the culture there was not conducive to teamwork. . . . They [the partners] diverted earnings from the firm in the form of swollen bonuses and dividends to themselves."[15] These comments were not made after Lehman's failure in 2008. They come from John Whitehead, then chairman of Goldman Sachs, Lehman's rival, commenting on the earlier difficulties of Lehman Brothers in 1984.[16] They explain why Goldman Sachs is still in business while Lehman is not. Lacking a corporate culture that valued the practice, as well as the profits, of banking, Lehman fell victim to the profit seeking it extolled.

Everyday experience tells us that while greed is a human motive, it is not, for most, a dominant one. We enjoy the kindness of strangers just as we benefit from dedicated teachers and devoted nurses. Most people work not only for material rewards but also for the satisfaction of the job and the respect of friends and colleagues. Greed is not generally an overriding motive even for the very wealthy. For them, money is a mark of status, a register of achievement—or the by-product of a passion for power or for business. And while there are people who are obsessive in their greed, that obsession frequently destroys them or the organizations that attract them. The achievement of wealth, like the attainment of happiness, is an oblique process, and the overly direct approach frequently ends in the bankruptcy courts—or the criminal ones.

Chapter 5

OBJECTIVES, GOALS AND ACTIONS—
How the Means Help Us
Discover the End

Uncertainty about the relationship between wealth and happiness has exercised humans for as long as any intellectual problem. According to Plutarch's account, King Croesus displayed his rich treasure hoards to Solon and asked if any man had been as fortunate. The truly fortunate man, replied Solon, was the honest Athenian, Tellus, who enjoyed his grandchildren and left his children well provided for when he died gloriously in battle. "We don't consider any man successful until he has died well."[1]

For Plutarch, to be fortunate was to live—and die—well. Aristotle wrote of *eudaimonia*, which is sometimes translated as *happiness* but more often as *flourishing*. Aristotle's concept, and the ethical system it implies, has influenced our thought for two millennia. But most philosophers and psychologists perceive a difference between happiness and *eudaimonia*.

The psychologist Daniel Nettle suggests that there are three broad senses of the term *happiness*.[2] The lowest—the basic level—comprises the momentary feelings that make us happy—the joy of sex, the pleasure of a beautiful sunset. The intermediate level is typically a state of mind rather than a physical response, a sense of satisfaction and well-being. These states of mind involve judgments about feelings as distinct from the feelings themselves. *Eudaimonia* is a high-level concept, a measure of quality of life, of flourishing, of fulfilling one's potential. Similar distinctions and taxonomies are used by other writers.[3]

Recognizing these different levels of happiness makes sense of the seemingly contradictory things that mountaineers, or parents, may tell us. The climber who reaches the summit of Everest has endured extreme discomfort (at the basic level) but on completion achieves a state of well-being (at the intermediate level) that, in conjunction with other achievements, may contribute to a life lived to the full (high level). Parenthood is, for many people, their most worthwhile accomplishment (high level). Parents derive a continuing sense of satisfaction (intermediate level) that is more than the sum of their transitory experiences of frustration and joy (basic level).

An old story tells of a visitor who encounters three stonemasons working on a medieval cathedral and asks each what he is doing. "I am cutting this stone to shape," says the first, describing his basic actions. "I am building a great cathedral," says the second, describing his intermediate goal. "And I am working for the glory of God," says the third, describing his high-level objective. The construction of architectural masterpieces required that high objectives be pursued through lesser, but nonetheless fulfilling, goals and actions.

The identification of high-level objectives, intermediate goals and basic actions is relevant in many contexts. Actions are associated with momentary feelings, and we use words like *pleasure*, *efficiency*, *reward* to describe them. Intermediate states and goals are described in states and achievements, and we employ terms such as *wealth* and *welfare*.

High-level objectives are accomplishments like personal flourishing and fulfillment, the sustenance of a great society, the creation of a fine business. For high-level objectives, we use language such as *fulfillment*, *greatness*, *excellence*, *goodness*. Intermediate states and goals are wealth, a contented home life or profit. Actions are taking a new job or playing with one's children, introducing new products or reducing the size of the workforce.

High-level objectives are typically loose and unquantifiable—though this does not mean it is not evident whether or not they are being achieved. For Messner or Mallory, the objective was personal fulfillment. For Bill Allen or George Merck, the objective was the development of a fine business. For Brunelleschi and Picasso, the objective was great art. For the promoters of the Panama Canal, the objective was to improve shipping communications between East and West. All of these objectives could be achieved only by translating them into intermediate goals and states and thereby reducing them to specific tasks—to build the 747, to erect a dome, to establish a new line of commercial activity.

The objective was to facilitate trade links; the goal was to improve sea links between Atlantic and Pacific ports; a link through the narrow isthmus of Central America was a means to that end; an action was the building of the Panama Canal. The objective was the expansion of British power; the goal of greater influence in North America was to be achieved through the state of control of central Canada; the action was Wolfe's assault on Quebec. The objective was to maintain ICI's industrial leadership; the goal was the responsible commercial application of chemistry; a state needed for that goal was a sustainably profitable business; the action that resulted was the launch of a pharmaceutical division within the company.

To function, we have to break a high-level objective—such as living well—into goals and actions. When Jack Welch lauded obliquity, he went on to point out that the injunction "maximize shareholder value" is not a useful guide to executive action. "That's not a strategy that helps you know what to do when you come to work every day."[4] Building a cathedral seems a problem amenable to direct solution. Priests issue commissions, architects draw up plans, constructors put the stones in place. The problem seems to be determinate—we know the objective. The problem seems to be closed—we can define the possibilities open to us. The problem seems relatively simple—we understand the relationships between the different components.

If we know enough about such a problem—its objectives, its possibilities, its interactions—we do not have to worry about sharing our high-level objectives with those who are chiseling the stone. We can describe the problem comprehensively from the outset and hence specify appropriate actions. We can pay our agents bonuses and fire them when they fail to meet our targets. That is what Lenin, the modernist architects and the business process reengineers believed.

But they were wrong. The Soviet Union collapsed, the Pruitt-Igoe project was demolished and the people who transformed the business world were not the men who employed armies of reengineering consultants. The people who did transform the business world were those, like Google's Sergey Brin and Apple's Steve Jobs, who adopted a more oblique approach to business transformation. They chose to invent new businesses rather than reengineer old ones, they adapted and improvised endlessly and they carried employees and customers along with them on a wave of enthusiasm.

Direct approaches make a distinction between means and ends that often does not exist in reality. To live life well we surely experience satisfaction and well-being, and a sense of well-being entails moments of pleasure and joy. But the connections are not in one direction only. We experience pleasure and joy more fully in the context of overall well-being: We derive satisfaction from fulfillment in our work and our social life.

Messner would not have conquered Everest without the self-confidence that came from his high-level objectives. The cricketer and author Ed Smith expresses it well: "I am not saying that personal development is more important than winning; on the contrary, I am saying that enjoying the journey of self-discovery, by removing some of the pressure and *angst* associated with winning at all costs, is one way of helping you to win more often."[5] The phenomenon of failing by trying too hard is common in sport: Bob Rotella, author of *Golf Is Not a Game of Perfect*, explains that you can only swing well when you can swing without thinking about it. He made a career by persuading audiences that the principle has much wider application than golf.[6]

The successful completion of the cathedral required the simultaneous pursuit of interacting basic actions, intermediate goals and high-level objectives. The stonemasons worked better because they understood that they were engaged in a great endeavor and that God was glorified not just by the magnificence of the cathedral but by their own dedication. The goals and actions that are necessary for the achievement of high-level objectives are also, in their own right, objectives: That is why all three men were correct in their descriptions of what they were doing. Great cathedrals are built by an oblique process. Notre Dame took almost two centuries to complete, under a succession of architects, several of whom redesigned the conception in fundamental ways.

The builders lived in a world in which objectives are multidimensional and imprecise, and in which these high-level objectives are refined through the process of realizing intermediate goals and performing basic actions: a world influenced by the unpredictable consequences of interaction with other people and organizations; a world whose potential complexity defies precise analysis or calculation; a world suffused with uncertainty in which the specification of problems is inevitably incomplete.

In a business environment—or any other environment with these characteristics—decision making cannot proceed by defining objectives, analyzing them into goals and subsequently breaking them down into actions. No priest or politician, counselor or manager, has the capacity to do this—and those who claim to, like Le Corbusier or Lenin, have immense capacity to damage the complex systems they attempt to plan. In that imperfectly understood world, high-level objectives are best achieved by constantly balancing their incompatible and incommensurable components—through obliquity.

Chapter 6

THE UBIQUITY OF OBLIQUITY—
How Obliquity Is Relevant to Many
Aspects of Our Lives

Building cathedrals takes time. The Florentine cathedral of Santa Maria del Fiore was intended to have the largest dome of any modern building. The problem for over a century was that no one knew how to build it. According to Vasari in his *Lives of the Painters*,[1] Brunelleschi won the commission to complete the structure by challenging his rivals to stand an egg upright on a piece of marble. After they all failed, he simply tapped the shell down on the marble and stood the egg on its broken end. He went on to crack the problem of constructing the dome. When Brunelleschi's rivals pointed out that anyone could have solved the egg problem in that way, the architect replied that anyone could build his dome once they had seen his solution.

You don't have to believe this story to recognize the validity of its point. Brunelleschi just perceived problems differently.

His combination of obliquity and linearity is seen, literally and figuratively, in his greatest achievement—the discovery of perspective. He drew things as we see them, rather than as we know they are. That notion now seems obvious, but painters had represented the world differently for thousands of years.

Brunelleschi's skill lay in his original interpretation of the problem. Such obliquity of approach distinguishes the genius from the merely competent, the creative problem solver from the computer. The computer is very good at solving the problem we have specified and asked it to solve, but less useful when we are not quite sure what the problem is.

Obliquity has been a military tactic for a long time, and military genius often reframes problems in oblique ways. Americans speak a kind of English rather than a kind of French because General James Wolfe captured Quebec in 1759 and made the British Crown the dominant influence in North America. Eschewing more obvious lines of attack, Wolfe's men scaled the precipitous Heights of Abraham and so took the city from the unprepared defenders. The Germans defeated the Maginot Line by going around it. Japanese invaders bicycled through the Malayan jungle to capture Singapore, whose guns faced out to sea.

Like Brunelleschi, Wolfe and the German and Japanese high commands simply saw the problem differently. The solutions they found appeared oblique, but, as with Brunelleschi's egg, they seemed direct once identified. Directness was the product of obliquity.

Suppose you are organizing a tennis competition with fifty participants. What is the smallest number of matches you need schedule to find a winner? You might have twenty-five games in the first round, then twelve games in the second (giving one player a free ticket to round three) and so on. Or, better, you could have only eighteen matches in the first round. Then eighteen winners from the thirty-six players would join the remaining fourteen in round two.

Once you have planned two or three possible ways of organizing the competition, you will probably notice that there are always forty-nine matches. In a knockout competition every player, except the eventual winner, is defeated once and once only, so the number of matches is one less than the number of players. Iteration and experience lead us to the best principles of analysis. The oblique solution involves recasting the problem—often described as lateral thinking—and then it becomes direct.

The traditional job of the artist is to represent his subject—the view from the Grand Canal, the passion of Christ, the wife of an affluent patron. But the skill of the artist, like the talent of the poet, lies in the originality with which this goal is interpreted. Dürer's engraving is a memorably realistic picture of a hare. The artist's skill gives it a three-dimensional quality. It looks . . . like a hare.

But so does a photograph of a hare, and a photograph of a hare is not a good photograph simply because it looks like a hare. We do not judge the quality of either a picture or a photograph of a hare by deciding how closely it resembles a hare. Even a rank amateur can take a photograph of which we will say: "That looks like a hare."

Sir Ernst Gombrich's famous introduction to art contrasts Dürer's work with animal representations by other painters.[2] Picasso adopted an oblique approach to a similar brief. His

The Young Hare by Albrecht Dürer
Superstock

The Cock by Pablo Picasso
Private collection/James Goodman Gallery,
New York, USA/Bridgeman

cockerel looks nothing like a photograph of a cockerel, yet Picasso's drawing captures the aggression and stupidity of a cockerel better than any photograph.

Picasso could have attacked his problem directly. He could certainly have drawn a realistic picture of a cockerel if he had wanted. But unlike Dürer, he did not attempt a representation of photographic quality. "Art," said Picasso, "is a lie that makes us realize the truth."[3] Not only did Picasso approach his objective obliquely: He had to. If his drawings had been photographically representational, what he produced would not have been seen as original work, nor Picasso as a great artist.

Perhaps all artists have a common high-level objective, such as *eudaimonia*. But individual artists translate this into more particular goals in different ways. Most pre-Renaissance European art was created to glorify God; Rembrandt was (a financially unsuccessful) CEO of a portrait-painting business; van Gogh simply wanted to paint and never earned a penny from his pictures; Picasso used his art as a means of access to wine and women. These more specific goals are in turn translated into particular activities—to portray the passion of Christ, to represent the sitter or please her husband, to realize a particular interpretation of a cathedral. These activities are accomplished through basic actions—the pencil strokes by which Picasso's technical skill realized his conception.

The oblique solution of complex problems is a matter of managing the interrelationships between the interpretation of high-level objectives, the realization of intermediate states and goals and the performance of basic actions. Such skillful interpretation is required in even the simplest problem.

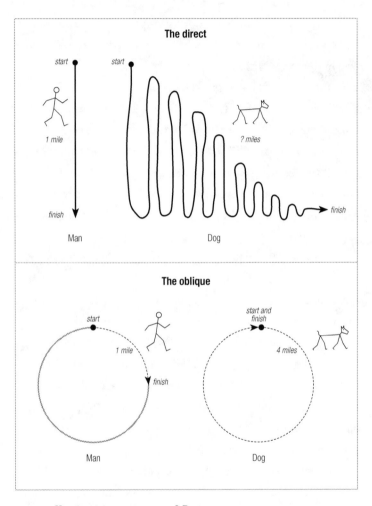

HOW FAR DOES THE DOG RUN? DIRECT AND OBLIQUE SOLUTIONS
Sue Lamble

A well-known brainteaser involves a man walking the mile
home from his office. As he sets off, his affectionate dog leaves
home to meet him, and when it does so, it licks his hand and
returns home. It repeats the process of running from home to

meet its master again and again until finally dog and master arrive home together. If the man walks three miles per hour, and the dog twelve miles per hour, how far does the dog run?

Most people approach this problem by calculating, correctly, that the dog first meets its owner after he has walked one-fifth of a mile—and so on. You can easily calculate the answer this way, at least if you know about the math of infinite series. But it is simpler to note that if the dog runs four times as fast as the man walks, the dog will have run four miles.

The oblique solution complicates the problem to simplify it: The direct solution is inefficient, the oblique more direct. Invented puzzles frequently have this paradoxical character. They are a response to the everyday pleasure we take in obliquity. Most people regard arithmetic as a boring task—they do not enjoy long division or calculating the square root of a large number—but many like mathematical puzzles. The most famous such problem—Fermat's Last Theorem—continues to intrigue. The 1994 proof by Andrew Wiles demands powerful computational tools.[4] But Fermat hinted at a simpler solution that has not yet been rediscovered. Perhaps there is an oblique approach that, like Brunelleschi's egg, or the presentation of perspective, or the Japanese assault on Singapore, is direct once thought of.

If we sometimes recast problems before we begin, more often we revise our specification in the process of actually tackling them. The National Park Service has learned to protect America's natural environment in the hundred years since it was established. One of the responsibilities of the service is forest management. We might agree, roughly, on the meaning of the objective of good forest management. That objective needs to be translated into intermediate goals necessary for the achievement of that high-level objective. A good forest is beautiful and accessible and has healthy trees.

One desirable intermediate state that contributes to these goals and objectives is the absence of destructive fires. From the early twentieth century, the policy of the NPS was one of zero tolerance. Every outbreak of fire, however small, would be extinguished—the basic-level action. But the incidence of fire did not fall: It increased.

Computer simulation of fire-control policies suggests the explanation. Most forest fires are small and burn themselves out. In doing so, they remove combustible undergrowth and create firebreaks that limit the spread of future fires. So the best way to reduce fire is not to extinguish all fires. The NPS adopted a different view of the goals that would achieve its higher-level objective: Controlled burning replaced zero tolerance. But what actions does this goal require? In 1972 the NPS decreed a new policy: It would put out man-made fires but allow natural ones to burn.

Sixteen years later, the largest fire in American history swept through Yellowstone National Park. In extremely dry conditions, several fires joined together. Lightning was probably the original cause, though perhaps arsonists lit some fires deliberately. By the time the blaze was controlled, by a force of twenty-five thousand firefighters at a cost of over one hundred million dollars, almost half the vegetation of the park had been destroyed.[5] Today's guidelines allow experienced forest rangers to use their judgment in deciding which fires should be tackled

and which left to burn. Experience has shown that too much ef-
fort devoted to fire extinction is counterproductive. But some
fire-control activity is essential.[6] Time demonstrates, but only
slowly, whether policy has gone too far in one direction or the
other—whether actions are appropriate to states, whether goals
are appropriate to objectives.

The complexity of the relationship between the whole and
the parts is an important reason why obliquity—the process of
adaptation and discovery—is, as it was for the foresters, the best
means of promoting the health of the whole. Yellowstone blazed,
and Lehman failed, because those who imposed direct solutions
to problems did not appreciate the complex relationships among
objectives, goals and actions. Extinguishing all fires made the
forest more vulnerable, and the bonus culture destroyed the organization that fostered it.

Obliquity recognizes the futility of reengineering, the im-
practicality of employing "serene and lucid minds" to conceive, as
Le Corbusier visualized, a plan that "ignored all current regula-
tions, all existing usages and channels." Le Corbusier developed
grandiose plans for the redevelopment of cities, most spectacu-
larly the Plan Voisin, which would have razed most of central Paris
to create a planned urban environment.[7]

This rebuilding never happened. But from the 1920s to
1968, the autocratic Robert Moses controlled the physical environment of New York, driving expressways directly where homes,
offices and factories had been only a short time before.[8] The
notion of the urban environment as a designed system was most
fully implemented in planned cities such as Brasília, Canberra

and Chandigarh. But these places are dull. The vitality of real communities is not successfully imitated by setting out to create a vital community. As with housing projects, their very function-ality is dysfunctional.

Jane Jacobs, who led the reaction against such planning (especially that of Moses), explained how the richness of city life was the product of obliquity, not design. Applauding Stanley Tankel's comment that "it is beyond the scope of anyone's imag-ination to create a community," she wrote scathingly of the plan-ners' approach to civic design: "Only an unimaginative man would think he could: only an arrogant man would want to."[9]

Both the tennis competition and the man-and-dog prob-lem have best solution methods. Both problems are easy, even though the best solution is not the obvious one. But once you know the best solution method, it is obvious that the particular oblique solution method you have discovered is best. In science and mathematics, there are sometimes eureka moments, after the famous if apocryphal occasion when Archimedes jumped from his bath having discovered the principle of displacement. But even these flashes of inspiration, in which a solution sud-denly reveals itself, generally come to people who have been thinking about a problem obliquely for a long time.

The nineteenth-century French scientist Louis Pasteur made numerous important scientific discoveries, including that of immunization based on artificial tissue cultures. His method of discovery was oblique: Pasteur observed the effect when a botched experiment by his assistant produced unexpected re-sults. That fortunate accident anticipated the similar obliquity of the most important of all pharmacological discoveries, that of penicillin. Pasteur's pioneering innovation was not even an intermediate goal. The invention of immunization was a means of realizing the high-level objective—the advance of scientific knowledge—that was made possible by an open process of experiment and adaptation. "Fortune," Pasteur observed, "favors the prepared mind."[10]

PART TWO

The Need for Obliquity: Why We Often Can't Solve Problems Directly

Chapter 7

MUDDLING THROUGH—
Why Oblique Approaches Succeed

In 1959, Charles Lindblom described "the science of muddling through." He contrasted two modes of decision making. The root, rational, comprehensive method was direct and involved a single comprehensive evaluation of all options in light of defined objectives. The oblique approach was characterized by what he called successive limited comparison. Lindblom described this process as "the science of muddling through."

"Muddling through" was a process of "initially building out from the current situation, step-by-step and by small degrees." Lindblom contrasted muddling through with a more direct approach, but unfavorably. "The root method, the 'best' way as a blueprint or model, is in fact not usable for complex policy questions, and administrators are forced to use the method of successive limited comparison."[1]

I first encountered Lindblom's article in a collection of readings on business strategy edited by Dr. H. Igor Ansoff.[2] But Dr. Ansoff included Lindblom's essay mainly to poke fun at it. He asserted that Lindblom "is wrong when he claims the 'root' method to be 'impossible': this is demonstrated by the third reading in the section (and further demonstrated in later sections)." He went on to say: "The TRW reading shows how one of the world's most dynamic corporations goes about a methodical exploration of wide vistas of opportunities in the process of formulating its corporate strategy. Nevertheless, Lindblom's article is instructive, since it describes a widely prevalent state of practice in business and government organisations."[3] When I first read Lindblom's article, I chortled along with Ansoff at Lindblom's antediluvian thinking.

TRW was not the only company to win plaudits from Dr. H. Igor Ansoff. His book contains case studies of several companies, among them Singer and ICI (!). But Dr. Ansoff's favorite was Litton Industries—"a proverbial success story by any conceivable yardstick," "the result of unremitting restless search for change."[4] Robert Heller was the British author of the Litton case study, and Heller observed that "every so often one particular American company acquires in British eyes a legendary reputation, a shining status as a management enterprise."[5] In 1968 that company was Litton.

The French glass and building products company Saint-Gobain was contrasted unfavorably with Litton and TRW. "One [director] who always comes to important meetings can't even stay awake. I tried to address myself to him, and there he was, fast asleep." "Saint-Gobain, for all the modernity of its headquarters building, will remain something of 'an old lady,' likely to move only with the slow deliberate steps of great age. The reason is not ignorance of what good management practice should be. . . . To a degree incomprehensible to Americans, Saint-Gobain must move through a veritable jungle of blood ties and corporate ties while carrying the dead weight of dozens of intracompany empires and three centuries of tradition."[6]

History has not served Dr. H. Igor Ansoff well. TRW, Singer and Litton all pursued similar strategies of poorly managed diversification that subsequently fell apart. Litton's legendary reputation survived the publication of Dr. Ansoff's work by less than a year. Singer and Litton are no longer independent companies and TRW is, once again, an automotive parts supplier of modest scale and ambition. Saint-Gobain, by contrast, is one of the most successful industrial companies in France and globally, with two hundred thousand employees worldwide.[7]

As Dr. Ansoff's heroes flew too close to the sun, Dr. Lindblom would celebrate the twentieth anniversary of his original article with a reiteration of his thesis, "Still Muddling, Not Yet Through."[8] Lindblom's thesis was that practical decision making is necessarily oblique. Such an approach, he says, involves no sharp distinction between means and ends and drastically limits analysis by problem simplification and by ignoring many potentially available options.

"The test of a 'good' policy," Lindblom claimed, "is typically that various analysts find themselves directly agreeing on a policy (without their agreeing that it is the most appropriate means to an agreed objective)." The modern legal scholar Cass Sunstein (President Obama's "regulatory czar") calls this "an incompletely theorized agreement."[9] Sunstein's insight is that decision making in politics, business and everyday life is often based on a common view of what to do that does not require a common view of the reasons for doing it.

The modesty of Lindblom's phrase *muddling through* invited Dr. Ansoff's scorn. The phrase involves intentional, but misleading, self-deprecation, and Ansoff fell into the trap. I think that *obliquity* is a better term. Obliquity is a process of experiment and discovery. Successes and failures and the expansion of knowledge lead to reassessment of our objectives and goals and the actions that result.

Oblique approaches to high-level objectives should not be equated with unstructured, "intuitive" decision making. Lindblom's vision of "muddling through" is a disciplined, ordered process. Picasso, Sam Walton, Buffett—each "muddled through," in Lindblom's sense. None relied on a root analysis of defined objectives. Each improvised, constantly. Each pursued a combination of high-level objectives, intermediate goals and basic actions. Each drastically limited the alternatives that were reviewed and relied on successive limited comparison rather than a comprehensive evaluation of all available options.

Just as Jack Welch did not sit at an empty desk wondering how next to maximize shareholder value, Picasso did not stare at a blank easel. His career is defined sequentially. There was his blue period, and then his cubist phase. In consecutive phases of his artistic development he explored a particular style, a group of subjects. Sam Walton opened his first store in Bentonville, Arkansas. Even today, the American Midwest is the center of gravity of the world's largest retailer, whose global headquarters is in Bentonville. It can safely be concluded that this site was not chosen after comprehensive evaluation of all options. Buffett has always emphasized his insistence on focusing on a small number of businesses and industries that he understands. Picasso, Walton, Buffett—each made his selection from a much smaller range of options than those in principle available.

Objectives, goals, states, actions evolve together because learning about the nature of high-level goals is a never-ending process. The distinction between means and ends, which seems obvious and important in simple problem solving, is, as Lindblom explains, not central to practical decision making. The process in which well-defined and prioritized objectives are broken down into specific states and actions whose progress can be monitored and measured is not the reality of how people find fulfillment in their lives, create great art, establish great societies or build good businesses.

Through oblique methods, striving for high-level objectives by constant adaptation, Messner and Mallory found personal fulfillment, Allen and Merck built great—and profitable—businesses, Brunelleschi and Picasso transformed artistic representation, the builders of the Panama Canal revolutionized sea transport, Wolfe made Britain the dominant power in North America and ICI was Britain's leading industrial company for seventy years. Living well, building great businesses, pushing back the frontiers of art, linking America with Asia, establishing an empire: These are large and complex problems, best handled obliquely.

Sudoku is different. It requires solvers to fill in the numbers one through nine in each nine-square segment of a nine-by-nine grid. Computer programs, which can quickly crunch through all possible arrangements, will solve any sudoku problem on a desktop machine within seconds. The rules of sudoku are simple yet comprehensive. The contestant must deduce the (unique) solution devised by an omnipotent observer (the puzzle setter).

If the world were like sudoku, decision making could be tackled in an equally direct way. The characteristics of sudoku that make such an approach possible are:

- There is one and only one solution, and when it is identified we know that we have found it. Objectives are clear and constant.
- The play is not influenced by the responses of others to one's moves. Interactions with others, if they are relevant at all, are limited and controllable or predictable.
- There is a complete list of possible actions, and we know that all the potential actions we consider are in fact available to us. Even if we do not know what will happen in the future, we know the range of possibilities and can sensibly attach probabilities to them. The problem is closed.
- The number of alternative ways of filling in the boxes, although running into many millions, is nevertheless sufficiently small that all can, at least in principle, be evaluated. Complexity, even if extensive, is bounded.

The game of sudoku is closed, determinate and tractable and has a clear-cut objective.

Yet human brains are attuned to real problems, not artificial ones. Although we could solve sudoku directly, as a computer would, we nevertheless solve it obliquely (and this is the only way we might take any pleasure in its solution). The general strategy is to tackle problems by adaptively translating the objective into intermediate goals and states (completing blocks) and basic actions (finding individual numbers). That strategy iterates, adapts, retreats when attempted solutions prove less promising than they appear. The methods of analysis that come naturally to us are oblique, and we derive no pleasure from direct, mechanical approaches. Anyone who buys a computer program to solve a sudoku problem has missed the point of the game.

Chess is more complicated than sudoku. But not so much more. The range of possibilities is larger, but still finite. There is no room for doubt about whether a move is legal or a solution valid. The rules are fixed. They do not change after we have begun the game. We might agree to play by different rules, but then we would not be playing chess. Chess, as we will see, lies on the boundary between the kinds of problems that are best solved directly and those that demand oblique solutions.

In the chapters that follow, I'll describe the factors that make the world different from sudoku: the loose and multidimensional nature of our objectives, the subtleties of our interactions with others, our inability to specify completely the problems we face, the complexity of the systems we handle. I'll stress the limits of our capacity for abstraction.

Lindblom's contrast between the root approach of a single comprehensive evaluation and the method of successive limited comparison, the contrast between the direct and the oblique, polarizes what is inevitably a spectrum. It is best to follow a simple rule when playing tic-tac-toe (although I bet few people could articulate what the rule is) but best not to conduct romantic relationships by reference to textbooks (although some hints, such as "Look at your partner" might help smooth the course of young love). But most problems lie somewhere between those extremes.

PROBLEMS WE FACE

		The Direct	The Oblique
	Chapters		
Objectives and goals	8	High-level objectives are defined and clear and can be quantified.	High-level objectives are loosely defined and multidimensional.
		There is a clear distinction between high-level goals and the states and actions that make their achievement possible.	There is no clear distinction among objectives, goals, states and actions. We learn about the nature of high-level objectives by creating the states and performing the actions that contribute to their achievement.

Interactions	9	Interactions with others are limited and others' responses depend on the actions we take.	The outcomes of interactions with others depend not just on the actions we perform but also on the social context in which our actions are performed and on others' interpretation of them.
Complexity	10	The structure of the relationships among objectives, states, goals and actions is understood.	Knowledge of the structure of relationships among goals, states and actions is imperfect and acquired as the process goes on.
Problems are incomplete and uncertainty widespread	11	The range of options is fixed and known.	Only a limited number of options are identified or perceived as available. In defining objectives, closure means deciding what to bring in and what to leave out.
		Risks in the environment can be described probabilistically.	The environment is uncertain. Not only do we not know what will happen, but we do not know the range of events that might happen.

The table on page 74 contrasts some of the characteristics of direct and oblique approaches to decisions and problem solving. The more numerous the characteristics of the problem that fall into one category or the other, the more likely it is that effective decision making will be direct or oblique.

Where objectives are clear and simple and policy and implementation can readily be distinguished, when interactions with others are limited and predictable, when we are confident in our ability to specify completely the available options and the risks to our objectives, when we feel we understand the systems with which we deal, when we can feel confident in our abstractions, our approach can be more direct. In the chapters that follow, I'll describe the difficulties that arise when these conditions are not fulfilled. These difficulties render the root method impracticable, as Lindblom understood, and make oblique approaches necessary.

Chapter 8

PLURALISM—
Why There Is Usually More Than
One Answer to a Problem

If we enjoy brain teasers such as sudoku, it is because the objective is clear, there is a best means of achieving it and when we have found it we know that we have found it. The further appeal of the good puzzle is that although the problem seems susceptible to direct solution, that solution is difficult and an oblique approach works much better.

Most real-life problems have less clear descriptions. Our high-level objectives are loosely defined and cannot be completely broken down in advance into specific goals and actions. Good problem solving and decision making is necessarily oblique because in the process of solving problems we learn not just about strategies for achieving our high-level objectives but about the nature of the objectives themselves.

The creation of a sustainable business—a high-level

objective—calls for achieving a variety of intermediate goals—profitability, good products, motivated employees, customer satisfaction. In turn, these goals require a series of actions—cost reduction, pricing policies, product launches.

High-level objectives—live a fulfilling life, create a successful business, produce a distinguished work of art, glorify God—are almost always too imprecise for us to have any clear idea how to achieve them. That doesn't imply that these goals lack meaning or the capacity for realization. We understand their meaning and realize them by translating them into intermediate goals and actions; we interpret and reinterpret them as we gain knowledge about the environment in which we operate. That is why successful approaches are oblique rather than direct.

In Peter Weir's film *Dead Poets Society*, Robin Williams plays a charismatic teacher expected to use a poetry text written by Dr. J. Evans Pritchard.[1] The greatness of a poem, Pritchard explains, is measured as the product of its importance and its perfection. Williams incites his class to tear the pages from Pritchard's text and instead inspires his sullen pupils to an appreciation of literature.[2]

This is caricature. But it is too easy to jump to the conclusion that poetry and science do not mix, that poetry is oblique but science direct. We know what Dr. Pritchard is trying to do. He is trying to translate the high-level objective "write a great poem" into more specific goals—perfection of form and importance of subject matter. Williams's students can recognize—and might themselves aspire to—these goals.

The world that seems inevitably oblique—the world of poetry—is not without rules or criteria. Anthologists, among whom we find the most sophisticated literary critics and commentators, compile collections of the greatest poems, as for example Dame Helen Gardner did in her definitive anthology, *The New Oxford Book of English Verse*.[3] Citizens seek a fine education for their children; politicians seek to deliver it. A recent publication from the British Treasury explains that there are many aspects to education—vocational training, citizenship, emotional development. True: We need to translate the high-level objective—a fine education—into goals and actions that can guide the framers of a curriculum.

Direct approaches seek to break down high-level objectives in an ordered and orderly manner. So if you teach in a British school or university today, you will be subject to teaching-quality assessment. Teaching quality is defined as the relationship of the classroom experience to the intended learning outcomes. If you are already shuddering at the jargon of the educational administrator—as well you may—then you are premature. Good teaching really does consist of classroom experiences that generate intended learning outcomes.

But great teachers achieve those obliquely by creating what really are classroom experiences—lessons whose content and effects remain with us for life. There cannot have been a single viewer of *Dead Poets Society* who would not have loved to be taught by Robin Williams, who throws away the textbook and revels in obliquity. Or who is not appalled when the headmaster replaces Williams and takes the class through the pages of Dr. J. Evans Pritchard's text.

The Treasury authors are anxious to impose more structure on Williams's disorderly if inspirational classrooms. "Clear

prioritisation is essential," they go on to say.[4] But what might be
the origin or basis of such clear prioritization? Does one award
40 percent weight to citizenship, 20 percent to emotional development and so on? If so, what would be the measures of citizenship and emotional development to which these weights would
be applied? Who would decide the weights? Teachers, government ministers, parliament? Or perhaps "clear prioritisation"
means setting the criteria in order of importance—citizenship
comes first, emotional development second, or vice versa. How
would one decide when "enough" citizenship had been instilled
and it was permissible, indeed necessary, to move on to emotional development?

We discover what we mean by a good education, our high-
level objective, through an oblique process of achieving goals
and implementing actions. We—or our leaders—adapt. We see
that we have devoted too much attention, or maybe too little, to
the academic side of education. Perhaps prevailing values have
shifted, or priorities have changed, along with the demands of
the social and economic environment. Always, we are learning
more about what is and is not a good education by educating
children. Because the process of achieving high-level objectives
is necessarily iterative in this sense, the path to these objectives is bound to be oblique.

When you cannot measure something, said Lord Kelvin,
"your knowledge is of a meagre and unsatisfactory kind."[5] That
is the approach of Dr. Pritchard. The Treasury officials who argued that "clear prioritisation is essential" followed this maxim.
But Kelvin was wrong. What Solon and Aristotle knew about
human flourishing, or Dame Helen Gardner knew about poetry,

was not meager or unsatisfactory; it is the Pritchard view of poetry that deserves these adjectives.

Kelvin's approach leads directly to the modern curse of bogus quantification. The United Nations produces an index of human development (HDI; see below), under which countries are ranked from Iceland (at the top) to Sierra Leone (at the bottom).[6] The high-level objective of human development is translated into three goals or states: longevity, educational standards and gross domestic product (GDP). The longevity measure, for example, takes life expectancy at birth (L) and then calculates $(L-25)/60$, so that if life expectancy is 82 years the score is 0.95. The educational score is the average of the literacy rate (with a weight of two-thirds) and the educational enrollment rate (with a weight of one-third). The overall score is calculated by averaging the scores on the three intermediate states.

Human Development Assessed

The Direct

$$\frac{1}{3}\left(\frac{L-25}{60}\right) + \frac{1}{3}\left(\frac{2}{3}*\frac{R}{99} + \frac{1}{3}F\right) + \frac{1}{3}\left(\frac{\cdots}{\cdots}\right)$$

United Nations HDI[7] =

$$\frac{1}{3}\left(\frac{L-25}{60}\right) + \frac{1}{3}\left(\frac{2}{3}*\frac{R}{99} + \frac{1}{3}E\right) + \frac{1}{3}\left(\frac{\cdots}{\cdots}\right)$$

The Oblique

"What is the highest good in all matters of action? As to the name, there is almost complete agreement, for uneducated and educated alike call it flourishing, and make flourishing identical with the good life and successful living. They disagree, however, about the meaning of flourishing."[8]

—Aristotle

The intentions are admirable. But why should we measure human development in this particular way? Some people might suggest that a measure of human development should include personal freedom, or the strength of religious belief (or its absence), or environmental awareness. Why? Or why not? Even if we agree that health, education and income are the relevant criteria, should we measure them in this way, and weight them in this way? Why? Or why not? The problem is not just that these are questions on which people might disagree. The problem is that it is difficult to see any criteria by which their disagreements might be resolved. The supposed objectivity of the measurement of human development—which is calculated to three decimal places—is spurious. Perhaps in this, as in so many things, Aristotle put it better.

There is today a substantial industry preparing similar arbitrary indices. The annual rankings of national competitiveness, published by the World Economic Forum and the business school IMD, receive a lot of attention, as do various rankings of the status of international universities. You can consult the happy planet index or assessments of human freedom. These tables tell us something. Most people would agree that Canada scores higher for human development than Sierra Leone. But if the index didn't give us that ranking, we would change the index, not our view of Canada or Sierra Leone. Our judgments of what is a great poem and what is meant by *human development* determine the measures and the weights, rather than the weights and measures determining our assessment of the greatness of the poem or the meaning of *human development*.

But surely business is still different from poetry, or sociology? If we must be subtle and oblique in our appreciation of poetry or our assessment of human development, we must be direct and linear in the measurement of profit. Profit is a fact. Or is it? If you look at a corporate annual report, you will find several different measures of profit. Very few companies headline the supposedly objective measures given by International Financial Reporting Standards (IFRS) or Generally Accepted Accounting Principles (GAAP), and for good reason. The financially oriented ICI aimed to "maximise value for our shareholders" while Phil Condit's Boeing focused on return on investment. Shareholder value and return on investment are not the same thing, and neither is the same as profit, as defined by IFRS or GAAP or any other standard.

That observation may surprise people unfamiliar with accounting and finance. Most people outside the business world—and many within it—think there is some "true" measure of profit out there, if only people worked hard enough to find it. But anyone who has thought hard about the matter knows that the quest for the true measure of profit is as illusory as the search for a measure of poetic perfection, and for essentially similar reasons. (I wrote a book two decades ago entitled *The Economic Analysis of Accounting Profitability*,[9] and I didn't find the holy grail then, or since.)

As we study business, we learn what is meant by *profit*, its multiplicity of meanings and the difficulties of interpreting what we mean by *profit*. As we read poetry, we learn what is meant by *perfection of form* (which may or may not be what Dr. Pritchard means by *perfection of form*) and how much, or how little, it matters. One of the reasons Dame Helen is particularly well placed to assess perfection of form is that she has read a lot of poetry. Her knowledge and judgment help us appreciate what is good poetry. The people who constructed GAAP and IFRS are highly experienced accountants who have struggled for many years and in many businesses with the appropriate definition of the financial state of the firm. The definition of these standards and principles requires, we find, many volumes. In many other areas of life, including finance, the existence of many different ways of describing an underlying concept means that we can choose between them only through our attempt to realize it.

In the face of such difficulties, the philosopher of ideas Isaiah Berlin wrote in support of value pluralism.[10] Berlin was concerned with lofty ideals of freedom and justice, not the more mundane problems of ranking poems for perfection of form or constructing balance sheets. In his quest, he envisages a multiplicity of social and political goals that are neither wholly incompatible nor wholly consistent with one another. Free societies are often just, but sometimes the demands of fairness conflict with personal or social liberty. You may have to compress the lecture on citizenship to promote emotional development.

Berlin sees the various social and political goals that give rise to a flourishing society as incommensurable. Dr. J. Evans Pritchard may be on the right track when he invites students to consider the importance of a poem's subject matter and the perfection of its form but on quite the wrong track when he proposes to measure greatness as the product of the two. It is not absurd to ask, "What are the characteristics of a great poem?" But it is absurd to ask whether Keats's "On First Looking into Chapman's Homer" is a greater poem than Whitman's "O Captain, My Captain," and if so how much greater. The goals of education are known, but the quest for clear prioritization of the incommensurable components of education misconceived.

Berlin's philosophy is pluralism, its essence "the notion that there is more than one answer to a question," in contrast to monism, "the ancient belief that there is a single harmony of truth into which everything, if it is genuine, must fit." Pluralism is naturally oblique in its approach to objectives, monism direct. For Berlin, there was no universal answer to the question "What is the nature of a good society?" Berlin is surely right to say that the question "How should I live?" like the question "What is the objective of education?" and so many others, has more than one answer.[11] The goals we struggle to attain are often incommensurable and even incompatible with one another.

We are rarely even sure exactly what these goals are, and the goals appropriate to our high-level objectives change over time. What is Dame Helen Gardner, the anthologist, looking for in a great poem? Writing in 1972, Dame Helen described her determination to choose "the best" and went on to assert, without equivocation, that Hopkins, Hardy, Yeats and Eliot were the finest English poets of the last hundred years. She was as ready as Dr. Pritchard to take a stand on what constituted greatness in a poem and on the qualities of greatness.

She differs from Dr. Pritchard not in purpose but in the erudition of her scholarship and the sophistication of her judgment. Her criteria seem to be a mixture of the subjective and the objective, the relativist and the absolute. "Any anthology that aims at being classic," Dame Helen claims, "will reflect not only the personal taste of the anthologist but also the critical consensus of the age." For the Victorians "best was either lyrical or epigrammatic not satirical, political, epistolary or didactic."[12] Not only do we lack fixed criteria of what constitutes greatness in poetry: To have such criteria would be to fail to recognize that freshness and originality are among the defining characteristics of great poetry.

Great artists do not only break the rules; they redefine them. Such obliquity is a key part of what makes a painter great. The great Dutch forger van Meegeren manufactured pictures that many experts mistook for original works of Rembrandt and Vermeer. Had they been original works of Rembrandt and Vermeer, we might have considered them distinguished paintings. As twentieth-century imitations, they are of slight artistic merit. Our criteria had changed, and although a modern copy may be a beautiful picture, it is not great art.[13]

The criteria that determine artistic success are ultimately determined by artists, not critics, and great art itself changes what these criteria are. Stalin attempted to define artistic merit in terms of socialist realism. The Nazis denounced art that was not directly representational as decadent. The attempt to define the quality of artistic endeavor by predetermined rules had the effect—and the intention—of freezing creative innovation. In consequence, little work of enduring merit emerged.[14]

What is true of art is also true of other areas of human endeavor. What made Henry Ford or Walt Disney or Steve Jobs great businessmen was that they modified the rules by which their success, and the success of others in their industry, were measured. They changed our appreciation of what is good and bad in personal transport, in children's entertainment, and in computing. They sold us products we had not imagined. What we mean today by *a good means of personal transport* is very different from what we would have meant by the same phrase a hundred and fifty years ago, as a result of people who conceived vehicles quite different from those that had already existed. The criteria of achievement are constantly redefined by great achievers.

Perhaps, at some very general level of definition, what we seek from art, or education, is also universal and unchanging. But to define objectives at such a high level is so ethereal as to be uninteresting and unhelpful. The task of interpreting an objective or a goal—such as a great painting or a good education—is not just part of the job of the good artist or teacher but the principal part. The definition of the objective or goal is not separable from the means by which that objective or goal is achieved, and that is why an oblique approach is not only effective but inevitable.

When we elect a government in a democratic society, we simply cast a ballot. We do not have to tell the government we reject why it has failed or the government we elect what we expect. We properly regard determining what we view as good government as a task of government itself. And the same is true of art or poetry or education or business—of any but the most mechanical tasks.

The job of the artist or the poet or the educator or the businessperson is not just to paint what we want to see, write what we want to read and hear, teach what we want to learn or produce what we want to buy. Their role is to interpret more fully than we could ourselves the underlying high-level objectives that we seek from art, poetry, education or goods and services. Success in recasting problems to achieve our objectives more fully than we had ourselves conceived distinguishes the great from the merely competent. And demonstrates why the direct approach is so often banal.

How should I live? What makes a poem great? What constitutes a good education or good business? We don't reach decisions about how to behave, what should go into a poem, what to teach or how to run a company as a result of performing some direct process that begins with abstract speculation about these large and general questions. We reach these decisions through an oblique process of negotiation, adaptation and compromise. As a result, these decisions will be resolved in different ways by different people at different times.

As Solon observed, only at the end will we know whether life was lived well. And whether we experienced a good education, whether business decisions were successful or whether the poem approached perfection of form is something that will be known only after, and often long after, the event. Even then we will never know whether the life that was lived or the education that was received, the business that was created or the poem that was written was the best possible.

No one will be buried with the epitaph "He maximized shareholder value," not just because the objective is an unworthy intermediate goal rather than a high-level objective but because, even with hindsight, no one can tell whether the goal of maximum shareholder value was achieved. If shareholder value was indeed maximized at ICI or Boeing, it was maximized obliquely.

The epitaph on men such as Henry Ford, or Bill Allen, or Walt Disney, or Steve Jobs reads instead: "He built a great business, which made money for shareholders, gave rewarding employment and stimulated the development of suppliers and distributors by meeting customers' needs that they had not known they had before these men developed products to satisfy them." Approaching high-level objectives in an oblique manner, they achieved many supporting goals.

Chapter 9

INTERACTION—
Why the Outcome of What We Do
Depends on How We Do It

The British department store chain Marks & Spencer was long famous for the breadth of its staff welfare program. The company gave its employees high-quality meals at low prices. But the policy did not originate in any direct calculation of costs and benefits; it was adopted when Simon Marks was making one of his legendary store visits. Marks discovered that the husband of the assistant serving him was unemployed and the family had not enough to eat. Marks was not engaged in philanthropy: He did not offer to feed his employee's family. But nor had he calculated how the policy might enhance shareholder value.

Marks was making a sincerely felt statement about the kind of business he wanted his company to be. Israel Sieff, Marks's deputy, described the late-night discussion that followed and focused on "the sense of participation, which cannot be supplied

by the best of wages or the most generous bonuses, but only by
signs of personal trust. . . . Welfare is something which is always
changing its opportunities and demands—because human nature and general circumstances are always changing."[1]

Marks and his colleagues had a rather general vision of the
business they wanted to build but were constantly adaptive in
decision making. Their chief method of market research was to
put goods on the shelves and see if they sold. Or not: Most of the
company's diversifications failed, with one unexpected success—
a food department. As a result, from the 1950s to the 1990s, fear
of Marks & Spencer was at the front of the mind of every other
UK retailer. But like ICI and Boeing, Marks & Spencer would sacrifice that status during the rationalist 1990s in the—ultimately
unsuccessful—pursuit of growth in earnings per share.[2] As at ICI
and Boeing, the oblique approach built shareholder value and
the direct approach destroyed it.

Since participation can only be stimulated "by signs of personal trust," how the company behaved in its interactions with
staff was particularly important. The statement "We look after
employees because we care" is not the same as the statement "We
have introduced new compensation arrangements because, having calculated the relative costs of benefits enhancements and
staff turnover and commissioned a consultant's report on the
policies of competitors, we believe our policy will produce a net
enhancement of shareholder value." Even if the pensions and
health-care benefits that result are the same, the response of
employees to the oblique approach is very different from the
response to the direct one. That is why companies often describe
their purposes in their board papers and investor presentations

in terms different from the language they use in press releases and in communications to employees. But people who work in a business generally know its nature well enough to see instrumentality at work.

Marks's approach defined the iconic company that Marks & Spencer became and the extraordinary loyalty it enjoyed from both staff and customers. Simon Marks was one of the most successful businessmen of his time, by every possible criterion. The business he dominated made large and increasing profits. Marks became a very wealthy man and he and his family noted philanthropists. Through its paternalistic treatment of employees, but at wages in line with its competitors', Marks & Spencer attracted the most capable workers. Management development was internally focused. Trainees tended either to find the culture suffocating and leave after a short time or to stay for life. As profits and returns continued to increase, no one complained about any lack of shareholder value. But this result was achieved obliquely.

The actions of the man who buys us a drink in the hope that we will buy his mutual funds are formally the same as those of the friend who buys us a drink because he likes our company. But it is usually not too difficult to spot the difference, and the difference matters. One way in which the difference matters is that we are more likely to buy the mutual fund from the friend. That is why the salesman adopted the oblique approach of giving us a drink rather than engaging in a direct pitch for his fund.

"Honesty is the best policy, a man who acts on that motive is not an honest man," wrote Archbishop Whately two centuries ago.[3] If we deal with someone for whom honesty is the best policy, we can never be sure that this is not the occasion on which, perhaps after many years, he or she will conclude that honesty is no longer the best policy. We do better to rely on people who are honest by character rather than honest by choice, because character is enduring and predictable, but policies are not. Marks & Spencer enjoyed exceptional loyalty from its staff for similar reasons. The welfare policy was adopted as a statement of values, not from calculation of consequences.

Oblique problem solving relies on constant experiment "because human nature and general circumstances are constantly changing" and it is only through experiment—putting new lines on the shelves—that we find out what they are. Such approaches demand diversity. The forests the National Park Service inherited were diverse, the product of thousands of years of unplanned development. In the nineteenth century, German foresters rejected unplanned evolution in favor of design. You can still see such planned forests in many countries of Europe and North America: The trees are identical and evenly spaced. The foresters have calculated the most suitable crop and the optimal planting distances.

These forests are generally ugly and were not very successful in economic terms, far more prone to accident and disease than the planters had anticipated. The foresters saw the trees but not the forest. You cannot necessarily deduce the properties of the whole by observing the properties of the individual parts. This is true of many biological systems and of all social, political and economic systems. Monocultures are vulnerable to both economic and natural hazards. Worse, they may breed such hazards. The Irish potato famine is the most famous example.

Planted in Ireland from the late seventeenth century, the potato proved wonderfully suitable for the local conditions. Potatoes grow readily in poor, damp soil and formed the basis of a nutritious if boring diet. The efficiency of the crop raised, and even appeared to remove, Malthusian limits to population growth in Ireland. The land could generate a surplus for the benefit of its English colonists.

Potato blight, like the potato itself, is thought to have originated in the Americas and arrived in Europe in 1843 and in Ireland in 1845. Potato growers suffered wherever potatoes were grown, but in Ireland, a nation of potato growers, they starved. Perhaps 20 percent of the Irish population died. The trickle of emigrants became a flood and the face of both Irish and British politics was changed forever.[4] Fewer people live on the island today than at the time of the famine. The goal of the Irish peasantry was subsistence in adverse conditions. They adopted a strategy for achieving this goal that would have been successful if pursued by one household alone but proved self-defeating when pursued by all. Ireland starved because of the interaction between the goals of individuals and the needs of society.

The planned, centralized solution failed in the forest because the planners did not possess the local knowledge held in communities that had nourished trees for thousands of years. The unplanned, decentralized solution failed in the Irish famine because the local communities did not possess the global knowledge required to anticipate, or protect against, potato blight. While decentralizing problem solving in society and in organizations is

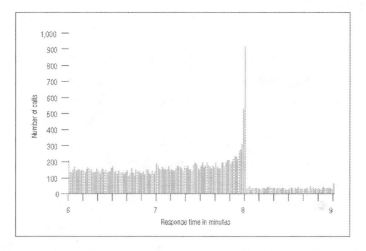

AMBULANCE RESPONSE TIMES
From Blastland and Dilnot

essential, the successful management of such decentralization is a complex process of iteration between central and local goals and central and local knowledge.

Central targeting, a technique of planners everywhere, regards such decentralization as an essentially mechanical problem—agents respond to stimuli as objects react to levers. Such principal/agent approaches, as they are called by economists, are sometimes a fruitful way of looking at the world. If you are clear about your objectives and sufficiently knowledgeable about the systems on which their achievement depends, then you can solve problems in this way. But objectives are often vague, complexity extensive, problem descriptions incomplete, the environment uncertain. And most important, responses change the nature of the problem itself.

When the British government imposed a target of "meeting

all life-threatening emergencies (category A) within eight min-utes,"[5] the outcome was as shown in figure 7, page 95.

We don't know whether the measurement was misleading. In normal circumstances, paramedics apply common sense in keeping records. But once bonuses and jobs depend on them, paramedics don't. (How exactly do the record keepers decide when the ambulance was requested or when the response ar-rived? Perhaps times a little over eight minutes were sometimes reported as a little under eight minutes. Perhaps the target had undesirable effects on behavior—dispatchers prioritized the calls they knew could be answered quickly at the expense of cases that were more difficult.) All we do know is that the introduction of measurement and control distorted the information needed to implement that measurement and control. This phenome-non is known as Goodhart's law,[6] after the British economist who observed that as soon as governments adopted monetary targets the aggregates they targeted changed their meaning and significance.

The story of the Soviet nail factory whose output target was based on the weight of nails it produced and was achieved by manufacturing a single giant nail is probably apocryphal. But the problem the story illustrates is entirely general. Of course, you can improve the result by refining the targets—you might pre-scribe the number of nails as well as their weight, for example. But they will probably still not provide the outcome you seek.

From 1987 the Basel agreements prescribed the amount of capital that banks must hold to support their lending and deposit-taking activities. These agreements do so in some detail—the accords of Basel II run to four hundred pages. The effect, we now realize, was to make banks riskier, not safer. Banks engaged in regulatory arbitrage—a mortgage-backed security might have a lower capital requirement than a mortgage, for example, even though the underlying risk was the same. Worse still, the targets relieved managers from making their own judgments. Since the crash of 2007–8, bankers who were paid millions a year have, with evident seriousness, blamed regulators for failing to impose sufficient constraints on their own risk taking.

Every attempt to decentralize processes must recognize that many intermediate goals will need to be achieved, and many basic actions performed, in the process of accomplishing high-level objectives, objectives that will themselves typically have many components. The balanced scorecard is one of the few business fads of the 1990s to have enduring value. The scorecard, which focuses attention not on one target but on many, reflecting many different aspects of corporate organization, recognizes the distorting effects of focusing on any single measure of performance. But Simon Marks and Israel Sieff realized that even multiplying the number of indicators was not enough. Complex high-level objectives could be decentralized effectively only if employees at every level absorbed the values that motivated these objectives. That decentralization not just of specific targets but of underlying values is what they achieved in their organization, and the powerful corporate culture that emerged is equally characteristic of many other successful businesses.

The stonemason committed to the glory of God will build a better cathedral than the stonemason who is motivated entirely

by the bonuses offered and scourges threatened by his employer. The executives, such as Bill Allen, who sought to build
great businesses established enduring competitive advantages
for their corporations. The executives at Citigroup and Lehman
who rewarded themselves with share options and "long-term"
incentive plans did not.

Chapter 10

COMPLEXITY—
How the World Is Too Complex for
Directness to Be Direct

Computers don't do obliquity. Computers work through pre-scribed routines of any degree of complexity in a direct, lin-ear manner with incredible speed and accuracy. Sudoku is an easy problem for a computer, and chess seems not much harder. At the dawn of the computer age, some people really believed that not just sudoku and chess but lives, loves and businesses could be efficiently run by computer.

Herbert Simon, a pioneer of artificial intelligence, wrote (in 1958) that:

> there are now in the world machines that think, that learn
> and that create. Moreover, their ability to do other things
> is going to increase rapidly until—in a visible future—the

range of problems they can handle will be coextensive with the range to which the human mind has been applied.[1]

Such a machine is the murderous computer HAL, star of Stanley Kubrick's film *2001: A Space Odyssey* (released in 1968). HAL was not merely a director's dream but the result of extensive consultation between the makers of the film and leading computer scientists of the time.[2] HAL's artificial intelligence would be the culmination of an Enlightenment project to bring to all areas of human endeavor the scientific principles that have solved so many issues in physics.

The scope of that project was set out by Benjamin Franklin, whose activities ranged from discovering electricity to helping to found the United States. In a famous letter to the English chemist Joseph Priestley, Franklin explained his rule for making decisions:

> Divide half a sheet of paper by a line into two columns; writing over the one <u>Pro</u>, and over the other <u>Con</u>. Then, during three or four days' consideration, I put down under the different heads short hints of the different motives, that at different times occur to me <u>for</u> or <u>against</u> the measure. When I have got them all together in one view, I endeavour to estimate the respective weights. . . . I have found great advantage for this kind of equation, in what may be called <u>moral</u> or <u>prudential algebra</u>.[3]

Appraisal systems in large organizations often follow Franklin's recommendation. When an employer appoints a person to a job or a bank approves a loan, when a civil servant presents an impact assessment of a policy proposal or a company board reviews the risks in the business, they frequently use a formal process that resembles Franklin's rule.

Charles Darwin attempted to follow Franklin's rule when he set out the pros and cons of marriage in two opposing columns. A wife would provide "children, companionship, the charms of music and female chit chat." She would be "an object to be beloved and played with"—though he did not seem to attach great weight to this, conceding only that a wife was in this respect "better than a dog anyhow."

But Darwin also noted the disadvantages of the married state: the prospect of "being forced to visit relatives, and to bend in every trifle"; the "loss of freedom to go where one liked, the conversation of clever men at clubs." At the time the great biologist had completed the fieldwork on his historic voyage to the Galapagos but had not yet completed *On the Origin of Species*. It is almost possible to sympathize when he underlines "terrible loss of time."

We snigger at the moral algebra of Franklin and Darwin. And so did they: Both men understood perfectly well that moral algebra is not how people really make decisions and that most people actually make judgments on more complex issues in oblique ways. Below his assessment Darwin scrawled: "It is intolerable to think of spending one's whole life, like a neuter bee, working, working—only picture to yourself a nice soft wife on a sofa." He ends his notes, "marry—marry—marry Q.E.D." The following year, he wedded Emma Wedgwood; the couple had ten children.[4]

Franklin knew that moral algebra was generally a rational-ization for a decision taken more obliquely. That is why as well as Franklin's rule he set out what I earlier called Franklin's gambit— "So convenient a thing is it to be a reasonable creature, since it enables one to find or make a reason for everything one had a mind to do."[5] The interview report, the loan proposal, the risk evaluation, are usually exemplifications of Franklin's gambit rather than Franklin's rule. They are written to rationalize the decision that has already been made.

Yet we think we ought to follow Franklin's rule. Perhaps a man actually decides to marry by imagining a picture of a nice soft wife on a sofa, rather than by a rigorous cost-benefit analy-sis. But this process is faulty. Surely we must make our best shot at moral algebra. We must learn as much as we can about the structure of relationships among goals, states and actions, even if we can't describe all possible options. Our knowledge of the world may be limited, but we should assemble all available in-formation and make estimates of the factors we do not know. We should use the most powerful computers and analytic capabili-ties to handle complexity. We should define our goals, focus on them and reward ourselves and others for progress toward them.

A postwar generation believed that the convergence of planning techniques and information technology opened un-limited horizons. In the Second World War the Soviet Union had massed its resources to play a key role in the defeat of Nazi Ger-many. Lenin may have been a dreamer, Stalin a monster, but under their centralized leadership an agricultural society was transformed into a powerful industrial state. Britain and the

United States imposed planning and direction on their wartime economies.

Allied work in code breaking led to the development of the computer. At the RAND Corporation in California, a group of formidably intelligent young men known as the Whiz Kids developed techniques of operations research. Their methods improved the logistics of the U.S. armed forces and suggested that computers could be used extensively in planning for the private sector.[6]

The Whiz Kids moved from government into business. "Tex" Thornton, their leader, sent Henry Ford II a telegram in 1945 offering the entire group's services. Ford's company was in a bad way. Henry senior, perhaps the most important business figure of the twentieth century, had become increasingly autocratic, irascible and erratic as he aged. The business urgently needed to reshape production for a peacetime economy.[7] Henry II hired the whole team. Its brightest member, Robert McNamara, was in due course appointed president of the company, but only for a few weeks before President Kennedy named him secretary of defense. The Ford Motor Company was by then an exemplar of management by numbers and analysis. Thornton, uncomfortable in Ford's bureaucracy, became chief executive of Litton Industries, the acquisitive conglomerate lionized by Dr. H. Igor Ansoff.

If the age of modernism ended at 3:32 P.M. on July 15, 1972, the era of moral algebra ended at 1:30 A.M. on January 31, 1968, with the bombardment of Saigon by the Vietcong. The Tet

Offensive would be a crushing military defeat for North Vietnam, which lost well over fifty thousand men and achieved none
of its principal military objectives. But in a classic illustration of
obliquity the apparently unsuccessful Tet Offensive secured ultimate victory for the North over the United States.[8]

Under McNamara's leadership, the Vietnam War had been
fought by numbers. How many opposition soldiers had been
killed? How many villages had been pacified? How far had the
enemy resources been depleted? You did not actually know the
answers to these questions, but you made the best estimates you
could. These best estimates were inevitably biased toward the
numbers your superiors wanted to hear.

A description of this obsession with quantification, however spurious the numbers, came from a frustrated colleague of
McNamara's at Ford.

> The bean counter wants to know all along the way how much
> is this, how much is that—and even before you get the gen-
> esis of the thing organized, they want to know the exact cost
> of each part. And you can't think that way, so what you do is
> lie, fake, hide things behind the blackboard. . . . They can
> always prove they are right. They've got it on paper. They
> are right, but they are wrong.[9]

Like Dr. J. Evans Pritchard, McNamara had gotten it on
paper. Like Dr. J. Evans Pritchard, he was right but he was wrong.
He was right in his attempt to provide a reasoned structure for
judgment and decision making; he was wrong in his belief that
their bogus quantification would help. Dr. Pritchard attempted

to quantify perfection of poetic form—a task that is simply impossible. The bean counters attempted to measure the demands of future motorists and the state of affairs in Vietnam. These tasks, less obviously infeasible, nevertheless demanded a far greater knowledge of the world than their proponents had or could ever aspire to. The mistake common to both processes is the belief that a number based on the flimsiest of data is better than a qualitative, and necessarily subjective, judgment.

At Ford and in Vietnam, their colleagues responded to the misapplication of Franklin's rule with Franklin's gambit. They made up the numbers to support the conclusions they believed their superiors wanted to reach. This was the process I exploited, profitably, in economic consultancy. The Tet Offensive, even though it failed, demonstrated the failure of the bean counters even more clearly. If the numbers that had been presented to the public had been right, the offensive could never have been mounted.

Within a few weeks of the Tet Offensive, McNamara was gone—to become president of the World Bank—and within the year Johnson would be driven from the presidency. It would be 1975 before the North Vietnamese finally captured Saigon, but their ultimate success was secured on that day in January.

If 1968 was a bad year for McNamara, it was also a bad year for Tex Thornton. The rise of Litton Industries, like everything that involved the Whiz Kids, depended on numbers, and Thornton had learned how to use numbers in imaginative ways. The heady rating attached to Litton's stock enabled the company to use that stock as currency for acquisitions, enhancing earnings and providing a springboard for the next acquisition. But when earnings faltered and comments on Thornton's stewardship ceased to be exclusively adulatory—as happened in 1968—the process started to unwind. Through the decade that followed, Litton would struggle to survive.[10]

The decline of Ford would prove a much lengthier process. Before 1968 the Japanese had arrived in the United States. The pioneer was Honda, which took the U.S. motorcycle industry by storm before turning its attention to cars. Honda established an American base that transformed the industry. The bikers of the 1950s had been hostile, rebellious characters of the kind portrayed by Marlon Brando in *The Wild One*. Honda's bestselling machine was the 50 cc Super Cub, its main distribution channel was sports shops and its advertising slogan was "You meet the nicest people on a Honda."[11]

There are two differing accounts of Honda's success. In one, prepared by the Boston Consulting Group, the achievement was direct: Having established an impregnable cost advantage in light machines in the Japanese domestic market, the company used that base as a launchpad for an attack on the U.S. market. Honda's victory would become the paradigm for Japanese global leadership in manufacturing.

An American business journalist, Richard Pascale, who interviewed the by-then-elderly Japanese who had brought Honda to the United States, told a very different, and decidedly oblique, story.[12] Pascale's account suggested the Japanese had assumed that only large and powerful bikes would be in demand in the wide open spaces of America. Honda imported its Super Cubs—a success in Japan—only because, cash strapped, the company's staff in America used them for personal transport around the cities and towns of California. The Super Cubs attracted wide attention—eventually that of a Sears buyer. The company distributed through sports shops because conventional bike dealers, mostly enthusiasts, looked askance at Japanese products: The "nicest people" tag was composed by a University of California undergraduate.

Neither of these stories is true. Honda has been too successful too often for accident and serendipity to provide a persuasive explanation of its success. Honda triumphed through improvisation and adaptation. The company's direct attack on established U.S. producers in their existing market segments failed. Honda did not expect there would be a U.S. demand for Super Cubs, but when the company learned of its mistake, it focused its efforts appropriately. When Honda encountered difficulty in accessing established bike distribution networks, it developed a new one in which it faced no competition. When a student came up with a good idea, Honda was ready to use it. The company destroyed its competition through an oblique attack that it did not plan—and probably could not have planned.

Robert McNamara was probably the most intelligent and skillful practitioner of analytic decision making to have occupied major positions in government and business. In retirement (he died in 2009), he would look back on a career of extraordinary distinction—and extraordinary failure. The Ford Motor Company would face a steady decline in the face of Japanese competition. McNamara would bear a heavy share of responsibility for America's failure in Vietnam. The expansion of lending by the World Bank during his tenure would prove to have done as much to fuel corruption as to promote development.

Of his greatest failure, Vietnam, McNamara would write:

> We misjudged then—as we have since—the geopolitical
> intentions of our adversaries, . . . We viewed the peo-
> ple and leaders of South Vietnam in terms of our own
> experience. . . . Our misjudgement of friend and foe alike
> reflected our profound ignorance of the history, culture,
> and politics of the people in the area, and the personalities
> and habits of their leaders.[13]

In Vietnam, McNamara's techniques failed because the
United States misunderstood the nature of the enemy's goals
and the means of achieving its own objectives. They were, in
McNamara's words, "profoundly ignorant" of the complex environment they faced. The greatest Whiz Kid of all simply did not
know enough—and never could have known enough—about the
people he was dealing with, the system he was challenging or the
environment in which he was operating—to use the techniques
of moral algebra that he and his colleagues had refined.

The Whiz Kids' methods worked for naval logistics, which
is a problem like sudoku: closed, complete, with understandable
goals and actions and little affected by individuals' reactions.
Applied to geopolitical events, or complex businesses, their
methods collapsed. These latter problems are best tackled not
by moral algebra but obliquely: They involve high-level objectives achieved through adaptation and iteration, with constant
rebalancing of incompatible and incommensurable components
that are imperfectly known but acquired as the process goes on.
Honda understood the power of obliquity; McNamara's Ford did
not. We see the results today.

Chapter 11

INCOMPLETENESS—
How We Rarely Know Enough About
the Nature of Our Problems

Almost all real problems are incompletely and imperfectly specified, and to tackle them we have to try to close them in some way. Closure means deciding what to bring in and what to leave out. Even when faced with what appear to be simple choices, we have to create our own description of the problems we try to solve.

Dame Helen Gardner was playing a literary game—to choose the best English poetry. But the rules of her game are not entirely clear. She encountered some difficulty—though perhaps surprisingly little—in deciding what was meant by *best*. The rules—the publisher's brief—required her to confine her choice to English verse. But what exactly was meant by *English verse*? She decided that the Duke of Orléans, Robert Burns and William Butler Yeats wrote English verse but Walt Whitman did not. I

suspect Dame Helen invented rules that would lead to that conclusion. She used Franklin's gambit—she found reasons for decisions already made.

Dame Helen's problem was incompletely specified when
the publisher gave her a commission, and she had to close the
problem herself. Different anthologists might have closed it in
a different way. Different anthologists did. The same publisher
had given the same commission fifty-three years earlier to Sir
Arthur Quiller-Couch (a Cambridge don who himself wrote poetry under the pen name Q)[1] and to Christopher Ricks[2] twenty-
seven years later, and each made a different selection.

Q and Ricks set different rules about which poets and
poems qualified for inclusion. It makes little sense for us to say
that one anthologist was right and the others wrong, although it
might make sense to say that one anthology was better than another. A problem can be closed in different ways, and some ways
may yield better results than others. Ford—who invented mass
production—and Disney—who reinvented the cartoon—closed
the problems they faced rather well. Among hundreds of automobile engineers and entrepreneurs, Ford created the product
and business model that would be the basis of the greatest new
industry of the twentieth century. Disney demonstrated how the
entertainment of children, which had occupied talented adults
for centuries, could be turned into a commercial activity of
global reach. That is how these men built great businesses and
became very rich.

If the executives of ICI and Boeing were to make decisions
about how to develop their business, they had to determine what
business it was. At ICI they thought their business was chemis-

try. The people at Boeing thought their business was airplanes. These companies might have defined these businesses more broadly or more narrowly. ICI might have believed the company was in agricultural products; Allen and colleagues might have taken the view that Boeing was a transportation company.

In a famous and widely cited article published in 1960, Theodore Levitt encouraged companies to view their business broadly. He suggested that railroads should have thought of their activity as transportation, not trains.[3] He encouraged oil companies to go into energy and buy coal mines. This didn't work out, but a few decades later the same companies built wind farms, for essentially similar reasons and very likely with similar results.

Most companies spend time discussing the question of what is their "core business." But to close that problem you have to define your categories. The Boston Consulting Group matrix provides a widely used framework that identifies businesses as stars, cows (to be milked) or dogs (to be kicked).[4] But I have never seen an analysis that didn't define the businesses the executives to whom the report was submitted liked as stars and the ones they didn't want as dogs. The analysts play Franklin's gambit.

Closing a problem means deciding what information should be discarded. It also means deciding which should be added. In even the simplest problem, our analysis is based on interpretation of the context. A problem deployed by experimental psychologists invites people to read, quickly, the words in the box.[5]

Many people will say "a bird in the hand." This is a mistake— or so the experimenter thinks. But who is really making the mistake: the pedant who offers the direct answer and reads "a bird in the the hand" or the person with a life, who approaches the

<small>A BIRD IN THE HAND?</small>
Sue Lamble

problem obliquely and valiantly finds sense in nonsense? Many of the experiments that purport to demonstrate our cognitive errors are of this kind. We bring the sensible processes we apply in daily life to wholly artificial, often absurd, situations whose design serves no purpose other than to provide scope for the purported error.

In problem solving, we bring to the task a cartload of common sense derived from nature and nurture. Juries are told to disregard everything but what they have heard at the trial, that they should close their minds to anything but the admitted evidence and the lawyers' arguments. But not only do juries fail to follow these strictures, we do not really want them to.

When a man is found with a bag of goods in a householder's garden at three o'clock in the morning, everyone knows the claim that he was there to return mislaid property is absurd. But how do we know this? That kind of information is what we call common sense, and people who lack it encounter serious difficulties in everyday life. The ability to make judgments of context is one of the skills that autistic people lack; they interpret prob-

The abstract version

All cards with animals on the front have an even number on the back.
Which cards must you turn over to ensure this rule is satisfied?

The concrete version

No one under 18 may drink alcohol.
What checks are required to ensure the law is being observed?

THE WASON TEST, PARTS 1 AND 2
Sue Lamble
Left to right: Bob Barkany, Juan Silva, DAJ, Image Source

lems literally. Working to rule—the refusal to apply common sense in interpreting the duties of employment—is notoriously disruptive.

An experiment devised forty years ago by the experimental psychologist Peter Wason to show the value of context has been repeated frequently since in different versions. Look at the two problems illustrated in figure 9 above.

Most people get the first (abstract and essentially mean-ingless) problem wrong. But the second (concrete) problem is easy. Yet both are the same. You need to turn over the two cards on the right, and it does not matter what is on the two cards on the left. We need to check that the card with a *3* has no animal on the back; that the alcoholic drink is not in the hands of someone under twenty-one; that the animal card does indeed have an even number; that the young girl is indeed consuming a soft drink. These checks are necessary and sufficient.

We solve these problems in an oblique manner, and that is why the problems, identical in their formal logic, do not seem identical to us. Our capacity to solve practical problems is greater than our facility with logical reasoning would suggest. Perhaps we may handle problems better if they are embedded in a social situation and if they involve enforcement of a rule. The context of the problem matters to our solution as much as the problem itself, so that our approach is intrinsically oblique.

Problems whose solutions require us to predict the future cannot, even in principle, be completely closed. Questions like "What will be the outcome of the Iraq war?" "What will be the economic consequences of China's rise?" or "How will economic and political systems deal with climate change?" are fundamentally and irretrievably open-ended. We cannot describe the range of outcomes in probabilistic terms, and decades from now there will still be disagreement over what the outcomes proved to be.

We suffer not just from ignorance of the future but also from a limited capacity to imagine what the future might be. People who are today concerned about the Iraq war, China's rise or climate change would not have been worrying about these issues twenty years ago. They would have been worrying about the cold war, Japan's economic preeminence and the effects of AIDS.

These earlier uncertainties have largely been resolved, and in ways that few people expected. But the key point is not that we mostly fail to anticipate the answers, rather that we mostly fail to anticipate the relevant questions. No one predicted the catastrophes of the twentieth century—the stalemate of the First World War, the influenza pandemic, the murder of millions of people by deranged dictators. Nor did many people anticipate the transforming political and economic developments of the century—the rise and fall of communism in Russia, decolonization, the development of information technology, the changed role of women in society.

Such failure of imagination is inevitable. If you could have anticipated the functions and uses of the personal computer, you would already have taken the main steps toward inventing it. To describe a future political movement or economic theory or line of philosophical thought is to bring it into existence. Most of what will be important in the future is outside our knowledge; it exists only in the future. The direct approach demands a capacity for prediction that we can never possess.

Chapter 12

ABSTRACTION—
Why Models Are Imperfect
Descriptions of Reality

Abstraction is the process of turning complex problems we cannot completely describe into simpler ones that we think we can solve. But gauging which simplification is appropriate requires judgment and experience. Our simplifications are idiosyncratic and subjective.

Before I knew London well, some friends invited me to a dinner party at their house in Hyde Park Gardens. They helpfully told me that the nearest Underground stop to their home was Lancaster Gate. The train to London arrived at Paddington Station. From there, as visitors to London tend to do, I took the subway and made the Underground trip from Paddington to Lancaster Gate. The relevant section of the map of the system shows this as a straightforward journey with a single change of

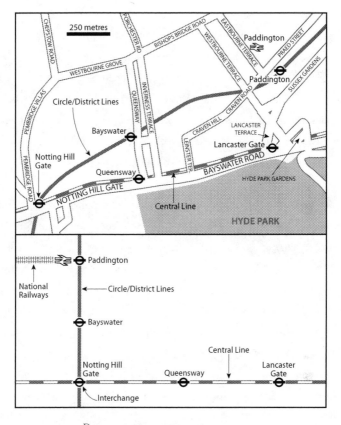

DIFFERENT MAPS FOR DIFFERENT NEEDS
ML Design

trains at Notting Hill Gate. The journey I made is shown in figure 10 above. My direct approach was very oblique indeed.

As I blushed with embarrassment while the dinner party laughed at my account of my trip, I vowed never to rely on the London Underground map again. But that map is widely, and justifiably, regarded as an inspired piece of graphic design. The map has been reprinted thousands of times and has guided millions of users successfully to their destinations.

Maps are familiar examples of decision-making models. They are, by design, simplified representations of complex reality. Jorge Luis Borges[1] tells the old story of the competition to devise the most perfect map of the world. The winners realized that the only way to represent the world with complete accuracy was to replicate the world, and the map they built was therefore useless.

The usual form of abstraction in business, finance and politics is the model. Like maps, models are selective simplifications. The idea is to approximate the indeterminate real problem with one that is completely determinate and simple enough to permit the computation of a correct answer. But—as in my journey to Hyde Park Gardens—the computed answer may be the correct answer to the problem in the model but the wrong answer to the problem in the world.

You arrive at a bus stop, and you believe that the service operates with a frequency of ten minutes. After several minutes, no bus has arrived. What should you do? A simple model helps with this decision. If the bus arrives at exactly ten-minute intervals, the probability that a bus will arrive in the next minute rises steadily with the length of time you have been waiting. The probability that it will come within a minute of your arrival is 0.1; after five minutes, the probability is 0.2; and after nine minutes, you can be perfectly certain the bus is about to arrive within a minute.

Of course, this model is crude. Not even the best-run bus company can make its buses arrive exactly ten minutes apart, and if the average interval is ten minutes you will sometimes have to wait eleven minutes. A more complex mathematical model can allow for randomness in actual arrival times, but a basic property of the simple model continues to hold: The longer you have already waited, the shorter the time you can expect to wait.

Many people, by the time they have waited some minutes, are no longer cool and relaxed in their confidence that the bus will come shortly: They are agitated, and by the time they have waited eleven or twelve minutes, they are more agitated still. For good reason. If the model is a good description of the world, their nervousness is unjustified. But after eleven minutes, they may reasonably start to wonder whether the model describes the world well. Perhaps they were misinformed about the schedule: Perhaps the route has changed. Perhaps there is a strike at the depot or an accident on the road. The list of reasons why the model might fail is long and necessarily incomplete. After some length of time—fifteen minutes, twenty, twenty-five—most people conclude that their model is, in fact, irrelevant and look for another route.

Anyone waiting at a bus stop is acting on a mental model that governs his or her decision. Perhaps only a sad mathematician would formalize it in the way I have outlined, but almost everyone appreciates the general properties of the model even if they have not spelled out the mathematics. The uncertainty about the bus's arrival has two components. There is risk derived from the randomness reproduced within the model: the known unknown. There is uncertainty about the appropriateness of the model as a description of the world: the unknown unknown. The first of these components allows an objective description; the second does not: There is not, and cannot be, any analysis that shows that it is right to wait for twenty minutes but wrong to wait for twenty-five.

When new data arrives—in this case, the information that the bus hasn't—we always have the problem of whether to treat it as new data about the parameters of the model or new data about the relevance of the model. The bus problem is tricky because these alternative interpretations of the data lead to quite different decisions. Within the model, the failure of a bus to arrive encourages you to wait. But the nonarrival of the bus encourages doubt about the relevance of the model in the first place.

In the first decade of the twenty-first century banks persuaded themselves that risk management could be treated as a problem that was closed, determinate and calculable—like working out when the bus will arrive. We, and they, learned that they were wrong. The most widely used template in the banking industry was called "value at risk" (VAR) and elaborated by JPMorgan. The bank published the details and subsequently spun off a business, RiskMetrics, which promotes it still.[2]

These risk models are based on analysis of the volatility of individual assets or asset classes and—crucially—on correlations, the relationships among the behaviors of different assets. The standard assumptions of most value-at-risk models are that the dispersion of investment returns follows the normal distribution, the bell curve that characterizes so many natural and social phenomena, and that future correlations will reproduce past ones.

The assumption of normal distribution of returns seems

to work well in times that are, well, normal. But what of abnormal times? The more sophisticated institutions test their own models against their own experience. But that experience is, of necessity, drawn from a period when the institution did not encounter the problems the models are designed to anticipate. The managers who used these models until their banks collapsed are like the people who are still waiting at the bus stop after an hour.

One thing we know with certainty about the banks, insurance companies and hedge funds that compete for our investments is that they did not go bust in the period from which their historical data is drawn. The risk models that financial institutions use ensure that it is very unlikely that these institutions will fail for the reasons that are incorporated into these models. That does not mean that they will not fail, only that if they fail it will be for other reasons. Which is, of course, what happened.

These abstractions are still relatively simple because, like sudoku, they don't involve response or interaction with the world. Chess has many of the characteristics of sudoku but also the substantial complication of an opponent who has a choice of moves.

Success of the direct approach to chess was much more elusive than the optimists of the 1960s had supposed. Finally, in 1997, a chess computer defeated the then world champion, Garry Kasparov. IBM, relieved, called it quits.[3] Even in chess, with a limited range of legal moves, the number of possible outcomes multiplies so rapidly that exhaustive calculation is beyond the scope of even the most powerful computer yet imagined. There is a formal procedure for describing such iterations called game theory, and its most basic solution concept—the Nash equilibrium—supposes

that each player adopts the best strategy available if the other
player does the same.

We can expect that there is a Nash equilibrium solution to
the game of chess, but we don't know what it is. In every game of
chess that has ever been played, there are moves for at least one
of the players that are better than the one played. Or to be exact,
we don't know for sure that there aren't. We wouldn't recognize
the perfect chess game even if we saw it played because we could
never be sure that neither player ever had a better move. It is
possible that white can always force a win at chess, or that black
can always achieve at least a draw. We don't know and it seems
inconceivable that we ever will.[4]

And curiously, it wouldn't help a chess player very much if
we did know. If you had a book that described the perfect chess
game, in which no move could ever be improved on, you would
begin your match against Kasparov by playing according to the
book. But Kasparov need only play one or two moves that are not
in the book. These are inferior moves, to be sure, but now the
book stops helping, and playing unaided against Kasparov, you
will need to be a grand master to stand even a chance. To guar-
antee a good result, the book would need to list the best response
to every possible move. But all the paper in the world would not
be enough to print such a book, nor all the electricity in the
world sufficient to power the computers needed to determine its
content.

Today the best computer can play chess about as well as the
best human. The best chess computers function by combining
the computational capacity of the machine with the professional
skills of a team of grand masters. Even a cheap computer pro-

gram will defeat an average player, but only because it is programmed with the skills of experts. The computer is an efficient decision-making aid, not an efficient decision maker.

In the ultimatum game, two people have to agree how to share one dollar; otherwise they receive nothing. There is an argument that you should accept anything you are offered—one cent is better than nothing—and because that is true for the other player also, you should demand ninety-nine cents. But that isn't what usually happens. In practice, many people reject low offers, even if the consequence is that they get nothing. Many trials of the game end very quickly with the two players agreeing to share the dollar.[5]

Why do people behave in these "irrational" ways? Only a few economists and game theorists find that question difficult. Everyone else knows that our approach to problem solving is more oblique. We are influenced by the context. We like the other person, or we want to develop a reputation as a tough negotiator. We feel angry at a derisory offer; we think that an equal division is fair.

The experimenters have tried to eliminate these subjective factors. They lock their subjects in a room where they can't see the other person. They tell them they only have to play the game once. They are trying to create a problem with defined objectives that is closed, simple and divorced from any social or economic context. What they are trying to do, of course, is to construct a problem to which the direct approach gives the correct answer.

They are substituting a problem their methods can solve for the problem we actually face. They think about their subjects as agents, or players, not people—and there is a big difference. We operate in a world in which we may sometimes be uncertain about our own objectives and will frequently be uncertain about the other player's objectives. Real ultimatum games only superficially resemble the experimenter's problem. These real-life problems are neither closed nor simple.

Even in an everyday ultimatum problem like negotiating a deal for a new car, we don't have the complete specification of the options available to us, and to the other player, that the ultimatum game provides. In a loose sense, we negotiate all the time—with our family and friends, our workmates, our employer. So we use oblique methods that depend on our interpretation of the context of the negotiations, and anger and a sense of fairness influence our responses to ultimatum problems.

Models are simplifications, and the appropriate simplifications are subjective. My failure with the London Underground map was not a failure in the map, or in my use of the map. The journey suggested by the map followed the best route by Underground from Paddington to Lancaster Gate; the map did not raise the question of whether it made sense to go by Underground from Paddington to Lancaster Gate at all. The model was not congruent with the problem, but without the knowledge of the wider context that the dinner-party guests had, and I lacked, there was no way of recognizing this.

Instead, I managed the problem badly. My approach was too direct, too overdesigned. I scanned the tube map from my study in Oxford and bought a through ticket that included my subway fare. If I had asked at Paddington for directions to Hyde Park Gardens, I would have saved much time: If I had tried to buy a subway ticket to Lancaster Gate, a kindly ticket clerk might have told me that this was a silly way to make that journey.

But computers are replacing these clerks. In 2009 I asked the Transport for London Web site how to get from Paddington Station to Hyde Park Gardens. It told me to take a bus in the opposite direction and then retrace the route of the bus on foot to Paddington Station. When I got off, I should walk directly to Hyde Park Gardens. There is an absurd logic to this proposal. The route is the quickest way to get from one location to the other by Transport for London bus. It is, of course, quicker still not to use the bus at all. The computer's ludicrously oblique solution is the direct answer to a badly formulated version of the problem.

PART THREE

Coping with Obliquity: How to Solve Problems in a Complex World

Chapter 13

THE FLICKERING LAMP OF HISTORY—
How We Mistakenly Infer
Design from Outcome

John Sculley was chief executive of Apple from 1983 to 1993. He gave an extended account of his tenure to *Newsweek* magazine,[1] which posed the question "From a champ to a chump?" Sculley's tenure included a period of great success—Apple's user-friendly mouse and desktop brought the personal computer within the capabilities of everyone. But Sculley's time at Apple also included a period of major failure—Microsoft achieved almost complete dominance of the industry. How could one man have been both so right and so wrong?

The magazine's analysis overlooked the obvious answer—that neither Apple's success nor its failure had much to do with Sculley, an able corporate bureaucrat who rode both up and down on the roller coaster of high technology. The Aristotelian Alasdair MacIntyre expresses it well:

One key reason why the presidents of large corporations do not control the United States is that they do not control their own corporations. . . . When implied organisational skill and power are deployed and the desired effect follows, all that we have witnessed is the same kind of sequence as that to be observed when a clergyman is fortunate enough to pray for rain just before the unpredicted end of a drought.[2]

We are inclined to see history through the lives of great men. That inclination blinds us to the real complexity of politics, business and finance. So we find intentionality and design where there is only chance and improvisation; directness where there is obliquity. By describing Napoleon's Russian campaign through the eyes of individual participants, Tolstoy denied the deterministic notion of history. Of the battle of Borodino, he wrote: "It was not Napoleon who directed the course of the battle, for none of his orders were carried out and during the battle he did not know what was going on. . . . It only seemed to Napoleon that it all took place by his will."[3]

"The mind-bending genius of David Beckham" was the headline in the *Daily Telegraph* on May 21, 2002. A few months earlier, the England footballer had scored a remarkable goal for England against Greece. Dr. Matt Carré, a specialist in computational fluid dynamics at the University of Sheffield, analyzed the process:

We know that the shot left his foot at 80 mph from 27 metres out, moved laterally over two metres during its flight

due to the amount of spin applied and during the last half
of its flight suddenly slowed to 42 mph, dipping into the top
corner of the goal. The sudden deceleration happens at the
moment when the airflow pattern around the ball changes
(from turbulent to laminar mode) increasing drag by more
than a hundred per cent.[4]

Dr. Carré went on to say that "Beckham was instinctively
applying some very sophisticated physics calculations to scoring
that great goal." But that statement doesn't make sense. Beckham isn't a physics genius. Whatever Beckham did, he didn't
solve a set of complex differential equations, in his head, on the
spur of the moment.

The human mind is programmed to look for patterns and
to seek causes, and this approach is often valuable. But that pro-
gramming leads us to see patterns in random events and to attribute intentions where none existed. We believe we observe
directness in obliquity. Sports fans believe in "hot hands," technical analysts think they can predict stock-market movements
by inspecting charts of past prices and fans and analysts con-
tinue to believe these things despite repeated demonstrations
that the runs of winning scores or the apparent pictures in the
data can be generated by chance.[5]

Nassim Nicholas Taleb describes how people in business and
finance are repeatedly "fooled by randomness," inferring skill
from runs of success although neither statistical analysis nor conversation with them reveals evidence of such skill.[6] Primitive peo-
ples believed that thunder and earthquakes were expressions of
the anger of the gods. Sophisticated and educated people routinely

anthropomorphize the planet, or Mr. Market. They mistakenly believe that things happen only because someone, somewhere, meant them to happen.

The teleological fallacy, which infers causes from outcomes, is one of the oldest mistakes people make. Today we are less inclined to make this error in observing the natural world, but in the business and political spheres the assumption that the good or bad outcome derives from good or bad design remains pervasive. This is how Tolstoy described it:

> The profoundest and most excellent dispositions and orders seem very bad, and every learned militarist criticizes them with looks of importance, when they relate to a battle that has been lost, and the very worst dispositions and orders seem very good and serious people fill whole volumes and demonstrate their merits, when they relate to a battle that has been won.[7]

Today we call these interpretations, and misinterpretations, halo effects.

ABB, the Swedish-Swiss engineering conglomerate, was lauded in the 1990s by business-school professors, consulting gurus and business journalists. In their gushing prose, ABB was the first truly transnational corporation, had invented a new organizational form, represented the "prototypical post-industrial organisation."[8] ABB was repeatedly voted Europe's most respected industrial company. Admiration for its chief executive, Percy Barnevik, ran ahead even of the ratings of the company.

In 2002 ABB's revenues and profits collapsed and the company struggled to survive under a mountain of debt. Now "the decentralised management structure Mr Barnevik created for the company's far-flung units ended up causing conflicts and communication problems between departments."[9] The qualities of charisma, boldness and vision that had once won plaudits for Barnevik were now portrayed as arrogance, aggression, resistance to criticism. Of course, neither ABB's organization nor Barnevik's personality had changed: What had changed was the company's results and hence the lens through which the organization and the personality were viewed.[10]

Similarly, Enron was considered a model of a new style of corporate organization when its stock price was rising and a hotbed of corporate corruption when it had gone bust. The financial innovation that until 2007 had been seen as a sophisticated way to spread and minimize risk was seen in 2008 as an unmanageable source of instability in the world financial system.

The mistake is to make inferences about the relationships between outcomes and processes when we cannot observe and do not understand the processes themselves. The battle of Borodino was a confused encounter between competing and dispersed armies with tens of thousands of men. The organization that was Enron spread its activities widely, and no chief executive could have controlled its operations, or did.

Solving equations of motion is a way to understand how well-judged shots find the goal but is not a way to make them happen. Successful firms may maximize long-term shareholder value, or at least create large quantities of it. But that does not

mean that these firms were any more capable of formally calculating the outcome of their activities than was Beckham, or that
attempting to emulate them will be any more rewarding than
emulating Beckham. In both cases, we don't know enough about
what they do for such emulation to succeed.

ICI might have made calculations in the 1950s that estimated the market capitalization its pharmaceutical division
could have achieved by the year 2000. The company could then
have put that number into a discounted-cash-flow calculation to
estimate a return on the company's early investment in its pharmaceutical business. I would have been delighted to build that
model for them. But no one would or should have taken such a
calculation seriously.

ICI could never have computed the likely effect of the company's initiative, but that does not mean the activity was random
or undirected. Far from it—it was an intelligent action in pursuit
of the high-level objective of the responsible application of
chemistry in industry. To say that intention cannot be inferred
from outcome is not to say that intentions have no effect on outcomes. Napoleon's influence on history may be exaggerated,
and Sculley may not have been the cause of Apple's success or
failure. But Napoleon did have an impact on the shape of modern Europe and Sculley bore responsibility for what happened
at Apple. Beckham certainly aimed to score his goal. Bill Allen
intended to build a great business and a profitable one. Wolfe
meant to capture Quebec and the Japanese certainly intended to
take Singapore.

In chapter seven I described a spectrum of problems. At

one end were those—like tic-tac-toe—best solved directly, at the other those—the pursuit of happiness—best achieved obliquely. There is an analogous spectrum of decision-making styles, from direct to oblique.

The direct decision maker perceives a direct connection between intentions and outcomes; the oblique decision maker believes that the intention is neither necessary nor sufficient to secure the outcome. The direct problem solver reviews all possible outcomes; the oblique problem solver chooses from a much more limited set. The direct problem solver assembles all available information; the oblique decision maker recognizes the limits of his or her knowledge. The direct decision maker maximizes his or her objectives; the oblique decision maker adapts continuously. The direct problem solver can always find an explanation for his or her choices; the oblique problem solver sometimes just finds the right answer. The direct decision maker believes that order is the production of a directing mind; the oblique decision maker recognizes that order often emerges spontaneously—no one fully grasps it. The direct problem solver insists on consistency, on always treating the same problem in the same way; the oblique problem solver never encounters exactly the same problem twice. The direct decision maker emphasizes the importance of rationality of process; the oblique decision maker believes that decision making is inherently subjective and prefers to emphasize good judgment. In the following chapters I review each of these issues in turn.

Oblique decision makers and problem solvers understand that the connection of intention and outcome is often not appar-

	Chapters	The Direct	The Oblique
Intentionality	13	What happens is what we intend to happen.	Outcomes arise through complex processes whose totality no one fully grasps.
Limited comparison	14	Actions are selected after scanning all available alternatives.	Actions are chosen from a constricted subset of options by successive limited comparison.
Information	15	Decisions are made on the basis of the fullest possible information.	Decisions are made after recognizing that only limited knowledge of the world is or can be available.
Eclecticism	15	Good decisions are made through explicit statement of objectives and a clear view of the world.	Good decision making is eclectic in its use of models, narratives and sources of evidence.
Adaptation	16	The best outcome is achieved through conscious processes of maximization.	Good outcomes are derived through continual (but often unsuccessful) adaptation to constantly changing circumstances.

Expertise	17	Rules can be defined that allow people (or machines) to find solutions.	The expert can do things that others can't—and can only rarely learn.
Direction	18	Order is achieved by a directing mind.	Order often emerges spontaneously.
Consistency	19	The rational decision maker is consistent.	Consistency is a minor, and possibly dangerous, virtue.
Process rationality	20	Good decisions are the product of a structured and careful process of calculation.	Good decisions are the outcome of good judgment.

ent either in prospect or retrospect. Hindsight colors our interpretations of events and history—and yet even with hindsight we often do not really understand either causes or outcomes. Neville Chamberlain returned from Munich proclaiming "peace in our time" and received a hero's welcome.[11] Eighteen months later he was driven from office, a broken man, and he died of cancer a few months after that. Winston Churchill delivered a characteristically powerful epitaph to the House of Commons:

> It is not given to human beings—happily for them, otherwise life would be intolerable—to foresee or predict to any large extent the unfolding of events. In one phase men seem to have been right, in another they seem to have been

wrong. Then again, a few years later, when the perspective of time has lengthened, all stands in a different setting. There is a new proportion. There is another scale of values. History with its flickering lamp stumbles along the trail of the past, trying to reconstruct its scenes, to revive its echoes.[12]

Chapter 14

THE STOCKDALE PARADOX—
How We Have Less Freedom of
Choice Than We Think

The oblique decision maker reviews only a small subset of the options in principle available. Napoleon did not direct the course of the battle of Borodino because for much of the time he did not know what was going on, and Sculley's position was little different. Beckham did not have time to review many alternatives before he kicked his goal.

Prisoners experience particularly severe constraints on their choices. Jim Collins, who observed the profit-seeking paradox, recounted an interview with Admiral James Stockdale. Stockdale was the most senior U.S. naval officer captured by the North Vietnamese and survived repeated torture and beatings before being released after seven years. (He ended his public career sadly as the inept vice-presidential nominee in Ross Perot's quixotic independent candidacy for the U.S. presidency in 1992.)

In Collins's account, Stockdale described the conditions of his survival. Collins emphasized Stockdale's determination to see his ordeal through, but also the pragmatism of his responses and the daily fatalism he demonstrated. Collins described this combination as the "Stockdale paradox."[1] Stockdale could remain confident of and committed to the high-level objective of survival, yet acknowledge that he had almost no freedom of choice about his current actions. A plan of how he would survive would have been harmful, not helpful. Stockdale observed that those who died were typically the optimists—those who said to themselves: "We'll be out by Christmas." Their spirits were broken by the continual frustration of their hopes.

A prisoner of brutal and arbitrary captors, Stockdale had unusually little control of his fate. But accounts similar to the Stockdale paradox are reported by survivors of other extreme experiences. One lesson from these great survivors is the realistic possibility of accomplishing high-level objectives even without knowledge of future states or control over current actions.

Roy Jenkins described the issue well: "Clutching at straws is only dangerous if, when they fail to offer support, the wishful thinker abandons resistance and sinks with them." Jenkins was describing the mood of Winston Churchill after becoming prime minister in 1940.[2] After the fall of France, Churchill reiterated his high-level objective for Britain—not just survival but victory. Yet neither Churchill nor any other British leader could have held any realistic conception of how that objective might be achieved.

A German invasion of Britain would have been a hazardous undertaking in many different ways, but a British attack on Europe without overwhelming assistance and support was inconceivable. Churchill understood that American participation in the war against Germany was a necessary condition of achieving his objective but did not have the capacity to bring that state about. The events that led to it—the German invasion of Russia and the Japanese attack on Pearl Harbor—could not realistically have been anticipated, and were not anticipated, when Churchill made his inspirational speeches in the summer of 1940.

Obliquity was forced on Stockdale and Churchill. But it is forced on all of us. The illusion that we have more control over our lives than we possess, that we understand more about the world and the future than we do or can, is pervasive. No position in the modern world carries more power and authority and greater scope to determine the environment within which the holder operates than the presidency of the United States. Surely presidents don't have to be oblique.

But they do. When Stockdale was captured, Lyndon Johnson was president. As Senate majority leader Johnson had been a master of obliquity, displaying Machiavellian aptitude in his ability to handle people and secure agreement.[3] But Johnson was trapped into an escalation of errors that divided his country. In turn, Richard Nixon, Johnson's successor and president when Stockdale was freed, also persisted in a course that compounded error on error until he could escape impeachment only by resignation.

Johnson and Nixon both enjoyed great power, yet still they overrated that power. They believed they could engineer a Great Society, or world peace, when in reality they were muddling through. They overestimated their authority and, imagining they were able to control their environment, failed to perceive how far their actions were constrained by their current realities. Having translated their high-level objectives into goals and actions, they became fixated on these goals and actions, even when the search for them had come to jeopardize rather than sustain their higher-level objectives.

Both Johnson and Nixon refused to acknowledge that the states they sought were unattainable long after this had grown clear to thoughtful people around them, like McNamara. For Johnson, success in Vietnam became an end in itself, and its unattainability destroyed his presidency. Nixon's obsession with his own reelection and advancement ultimately had the opposite of the intended effect. Misunderstanding their power, these men not only failed to achieve the intermediate goals to which they had given undue primacy—a victorious outcome in Vietnam, the crushing of Nixon's political opponents—but in consequence failed to achieve the higher-level objectives on which they were set.

The most successful twentieth-century U.S. president, Franklin D. Roosevelt, understood very well that goals and actions must constantly be revised if high-level objectives are to be achieved. Roosevelt described his approach as one of "bold, persistent experimentation." "Try something," Roosevelt went on. "If it fails, admit it frankly, and try another."[4]

Roosevelt's achievement was based on combining a strong general sense of high-level objectives with an equally marked absence of commitment to any specific intermediate or basic goals or actions. Two high-level objectives were formulated early in his presidency. He needed to broker enough compromises with business interests and market ideologies to secure the survival of American capitalism. And he was required to position his country for a conflict with the aggressive military powers of Germany and Japan. Roosevelt realized such conflict was likely long before his electorate or Congress was ready to contemplate the foreign engagements implied.

Roosevelt is admired today because he achieved these high-level objectives, but he did so through pragmatic improvisation in the face of circumstances that neither he nor his outstanding advisers could predict or control. The achievement of the greatest of nineteenth-century U.S. presidents, Abraham Lincoln, in preserving the Union is similar. Both Roosevelt and Lincoln understood that to approach their goals too directly would risk failure to achieve them. Their obliquity caused frustration to many around them, and to many historians who record their careers today. As we read a modern account of Roosevelt gently edging his country toward the inevitable war, we wonder constantly today: "Why doesn't he get on with it?" Roosevelt knew better. His goal could only be achieved if approached obliquely.

Roosevelt, like Lincoln before him, understood that the scope of his authority was inescapably limited by the imprecision of his objectives, the complexity of his environment, the unpredictability of the reactions of others and the open-ended nature of the problems he faced. All these factors mean that even the most powerful men in the world must proceed by choosing opportunistically from a narrow range of options.

Chapter 15

THE HEDGEHOG AND THE FOX—
How Good Decision Makers
Recognize the Limits of Their
Knowledge

The options these great men had available were limited not just by the scope of their authority but by their ignorance of what the options might be. Stockdale, Roosevelt and Churchill all had to make assumptions about the nature of the problem they faced. By the nature of his situation, Stockdale knew almost nothing. He could not follow the progress of the war of which he was a victim, nor did he learn of the events that would resolve it.

Roosevelt and Churchill knew as much as it was possible for them to know, and still it was far from enough. Hitler's Russian campaign and the Japanese assault on Pearl Harbor were the key events in turning Churchill's fortunes around, and both came as a surprise to him. They also came as a surprise to Stalin and Roosevelt, the men most directly involved, despite what we now believe to be clear warnings that these attacks were imminent. Even when these leaders had excellent intelligence, they misinterpreted it.

The decisions legendary financiers make—to buy 10 percent of the Coca-Cola Company, to sell sterling—are less momentous than decisions to invade Russia or bomb Hawaii. But if a single activity provides an objective test of the quality of personal decisions, it is the process of investment. Successful investment processes are frequently associated with single individuals. Such individuals make identifiable decisions—to buy and sell—frequently. They do so in competition with other people attempting to do more or less the same thing.

The two most successful investors of recent times are Warren Buffett—the man who bought 10 percent of Coca-Cola—and George Soros—who sold sterling in sufficient quantity to force the UK out of its shadowing of the European Monetary System. Their success has been sustained over a lengthy period and has continued to be sustained even after their talents have been widely recognized. Both are highly intelligent and articulate men who have written extensively about their approaches and methods. A striking feature of the accounts of both is a certain kind of modesty: their ready acknowledgment of their own ignorance and equally ready admission that they make mistakes. They are not modest in a broader sense—both are proud of their success, and neither is quiet about that success.

In many industries, of course, Charlie [Munger, Buffett's longtime business partner] and I can't determine whether we are dealing with a "pet rock" or a "Barbie." We wouldn't solve this problem, moreover, even if we were to spend years intensely studying these industries. Sometimes our own intellectual shortcomings would stand in the way of understanding, and in other cases the nature of the industry would be the road block.[1]

Buffett tries to live a life without surprises by confining his attention to a small number of problems he feels able to solve. But politicians and businesspeople rarely have this luxury. Soros, less reticent, recognizes his own ignorance:

> My financial success stands in stark contrast with my ability to forecast events. In this context, we must distinguish between events in financial markets and events in the real world. . . . Even in predicting financial markets my record is less than impressive: the best that can be said for it is that my theoretical framework enables me to understand the significance of events as they unfold—although the record is far from spotless. . . . With regard to events in the real world, my record is downright dismal. The outstanding feature of my predictions is that I keep on expecting developments that do not materialize.[2]

Both Buffett and Soros are decisive in their actions yet eclectic in their thought. In a famous essay, Isaiah Berlin adopted Tolstoy's distinction between the hedgehog—who knows one big thing—and the fox—who knows many little things. Hedgehogs move slowly and directly, foxes quickly and obliquely. There are important roles for both kinds of attribute. If Roosevelt was a fox, Churchill was a hedgehog, yet both were obviously great leaders: Roosevelt, like Lincoln, steered his country through troubled years, Churchill led his country to victory in its greatest crisis.[3]

The political scientist Philip Tetlock has used this taxonomy in a long-term study of expert political judgment.[4] Over two decades, he invited respondents to predict political events and used hindsight to assess the quality of their responses. The experts were not very good at anticipating the future. No surprise: The world is complex and uncertain; our understanding of it is incomplete.

But Tetlock's most striking discovery is that although the foxes perform better in terms of the quality of their judgments, the hedgehogs perform better in terms of public acclaim. Hedgehogs are people who know the answers. Foxes know the limitations of their knowledge. Hedgehogs create headlines for journalists, and their confident certainties attract the attention of politicians and business leaders. Give me a one-handed economist, goes the saying, but careful judgment really is often a matter of "on the one hand, and on the other." Yet explicit hedgehogs who claim to predict the future will always attract a larger audience than eclectic foxes who acknowledge they can't, even if the larger audience learns nothing useful from the predictions.

John Maynard Keynes described a conversation with Max Planck, in which the great physicist said he had eschewed economics because it was too difficult. Planck was intellectually a hedgehog, who won a Nobel Prize for his big idea; Keynes, by nature a fox. Keynes went on to explain that economic understanding required an amalgam of logic and intuition and a wide knowledge of facts, most of which are not precise: a requirement "overwhelmingly difficult for those whose gift mainly consists in the power to imagine and pursue to their furthest points the implications and prior condition of comparatively simple facts which are known with a high degree of precision."[5]

If Roosevelt was the most skilful of political foxes, Keynes was the greatest of intellectual foxes. The eclecticism of his knowledge and the breadth of his interests made him the finest commentator on economics and finance of the twentieth century. Keynes resisted any attempt to explain social and economic phenomena with one big idea.

In Keynes's lifetime the one big idea most commonly used by hedgehogs to provide a unified explanation of economic and political events was Marxist socialism. Later in the century, as the appeal of socialism crumbled with the failed regimes that claimed to implement it, other ideologies, such as market fundamentalism and environmentalism, arose to fill the gap.

But as Keynes emphasized in his exchange with Planck, most useful economic and political knowledge is simply not of this simple, universal kind. Churchill, the hedgehog, won his place in history by being presciently and ultimately triumphantly right about one big thing—perhaps the biggest thing of the twentieth century. But on other matters his judgment was poor, the causes he pursued to the point of failure misconceived: the ill-fated Gallipoli expedition of 1915 and the disastrous return to the gold standard ten years later, his quixotic support of the deposed Edward VIII in 1936 and his stubborn resistance to Indian independence.

When Jane Jacobs accused the modernist town planners of being unimaginative, she was making a subtle point. At first sight, visionaries who seek to rebuild whole cities seem engaged in extraordinary feats of imagination. But in reality, Le Corbusier's schemes were characterized by a few ideas pursued with obsession. No one could design a city of three million people in any other way. The creation of living cities demands a multiplicity of objectives. Interactions among people are critical; their organization is necessarily complex, our understanding of them incomplete. The planning of Le Corbusier, or Robert Moses, can only be based on crass simplification and repetition of familiar themes.

The same combination of simplification and reiteration is found in the thinking of gurus who believe they can reengineer large corporations, ideologues who see all political events through the same lens and visionaries who project some current technological or geopolitical trend with exaggerated pace and to exaggerated extent. All lack the real imagination needed to understand the complexity of their environment. Hedgehogs, not foxes, they strive toward answers that were formed in their minds even before they encountered the problem.

In Joseph Conrad's novella *Typhoon*, Captain MacWhirr is the pathologically unimaginative captain who insists on steaming directly into the face of a tropical storm—and bravely and skillfully steers his ship and his crew through it. MacWhirr makes no concession to obliquity: "All the rules for dodging breezes and circumventing the winds of heaven, Mr Jukes,

seem to me the maddest thing, when you come to look at it
sensibly."[6] (MacWhirr, notably, can conceive obliquity only in
terms of an alternative set of rules.)

MacWhirr explains, obliquely, why hedgehogs often receive more applause than foxes. He ponders the implications of
an oblique approach:

> Suppose I went swinging off my course and came in two
> days late, and they asked me "where have you been all
> that time, Captain?" What would I say to that? "Went round
> to dodge the bad weather", I would say. "It must been
> dam' bad", they would say. "I don't know, I've dodged
> clear of it".[7]

The hero is not the captain who sails obliquely round the
storm but the captain who takes his ship through it. The diplo-
mats who might have dissuaded an invasion of the Falklands
through oblique approaches would not have been congratulated
on their achievements, but the politicians who attacked the re-
sulting crisis directly were admired for their resolution. The
intelligence agents who anticipated an attack on the Twin Towers
were not praised for their prescience; the risk managers who
warned banks of impending nemesis were fired. It is good for
reputation to succeed against the odds. But it is often better for
reputation to fail against the odds than to improve them. In an
uncertain situation the effect of improving the odds is never obvious, either before the event or after it.

Captain MacWhirr, limited man though he was, understood
that dilemma. Machiavelli, the epitome of the oblique decision

maker, was the archetypal fox. Five centuries before Tetlock confirmed it empirically, Machiavelli understood that to be an effective decision maker it was wise not to seek public credit for the success of one's decisions. Yet another of obliquity's many paradoxes.

Chapter 16

THE BLIND WATCHMAKER—
How Adaptation Is Smarter
Than We Are

In our histories of the Second World War and of ICI, at Wembley Stadium or Borodino, we are inclined to ascribe the outcome to a process of calculation that never took place and never could have taken place. Perhaps the most famous exposition of the argument from design—that the complexity of the world can only possibly result from the intention of a creator—is that of the eighteenth-century theologian William Paley.[1]

Paley used the metaphor of a watch found on a heath to illustrate his argument. If we stumbled across such a complex instrument, we would immediately recognize that it could exist only as a result of deliberate action. Within a century, Darwin would throw Paley's metaphor back in his face. Unplanned evolution— the blind watchmaker, in Richard Dawkins's phrase[2]—could produce complexity beyond anything that humans, at least, could design or understand.

And yet the success of obliquity remains paradoxical. Surely you must do better if you intend to achieve something than if you don't? The metaphor of the blind watchmaker illustrates that the answer to that question is often *no*. If the environment is uncertain, imperfectly understood and constantly changing, the product of a process of adaptation and evolution may be better adapted to that environment than the product of conscious design. It generally will be.

Of course, there is no blind watchmaker. A common mistake—often made with Dawkins's even more famous metaphor, the selfish gene[3]—is to treat the metaphor literally. Metaphors and models only illustrate, and illustrate imperfectly. Genes are not in fact selfish—the idea of attributing conscious motivation to a gene is absurd. The claim made for the selfish gene is that evolution without design achieves results similar to those to that an omniscient advocate of the interests of the gene *might* have achieved. And results better than those that a normally competent advocate of the interests of the gene *would* have achieved.

In tropical waters around the world, cleaner fish remove parasites from the mouths of predators. The large fish attend "cleaning stations," and the smaller fish that congregate there swim into their jaws. Having performed a prophylactic service as they eat their meal, the small fish swim out again unharmed. This phenomenon is hard enough to imagine, let alone invent, and nobody did invent it.

What would a management consultant advise the predators

to do? A superficial assessment would lead to a recommendation that the predators eat the cleaners. And this conclusion might be right. The more sophisticated consultant would need to define and close the problem—how large a group of predator fish does he represent? Are their goals simply their own hygiene and nutrition? Do the predators have broader objectives: perhaps concerns for their reputation and the marine environment? The consultant would need to assess the available feeding alternatives, for both cleaners and predators. A proper report would need to take account of the subsequent effects on other marine species and the impact on predator welfare. Perhaps you can already envisage the PowerPoint presentation.

I don't know what the answer would be, although I am confident I could develop a model to deliver any answer I thought my client wanted. Perhaps you share my skepticism, however, about the value of such intervention in an environment in which there are multiple and conflicting objectives and an ecology of great complexity. It is very unlikely, in fact it is inconceivable, that reengineering—an answer to the question "If I were recreating this ecosystem today, given what I know and given current technology, what would it look like?"—would come up with something better. The only approach that might do that would be to try out incremental modifications and see if they worked—an oblique approach.

In complex systems, the blind watchmaker may be more effective than the sighted one. The ant colony is a social and economic organization of subtlety and complexity, and no one planned it. Small children judge the size and speed of an approaching object with an accuracy that complex optics and computers find hard to emulate. If there is a one-line explanation of the power of obliquity, it would be "Evolution is smarter than you are."

Evolutionary models show that complex organisms—well-ordered corporations, well-functioning societies, prosperous economies—*could* be produced without omniscience, not that they *were* produced without omniscience. So planners, business executives and political leaders who have such omniscient knowledge, or believe they do, have no need of obliquity. The rest of us, however, do.

In natural selection, the unit of selection is the gene, the process of modification is random, the vehicle of genetic propagation is the individual and there is little or no group selection or inheritance of acquired characteristics. This is the model that Darwin discovered and his successors have explicated.

But there are many different kinds of evolutionary processes. Their key characteristics are a tendency to repetition or replication, frequent modification through incremental change and a filtering mechanism that favors modifications that fit the environment. The processes of social and economic adaptation involve learning and imitation. Such adaptive processes operate on groups—firms and industries, nations, political parties and groups of friends—as well as on individuals. They operate on characteristics that have been acquired as well as on those that have been inherited. More generally, these different mechanisms of evolution and adaptation operate much faster than the natural selection of species over many generations. Perhaps there is a better one-sentence resolution of the paradox of obliquity—"Adaptation is smarter than you are."

Most of the world's adult population is unable to digest lactose, an enzyme found in fresh milk, and finds fresh milk unpalatable. If this surprises you, the reason is that you function within a limited set of friends and acquaintances. Most people in northwest Europe, and the descendants of immigrants from northwest Europe, are lactose tolerant. The wet, temperate climate of northwest Europe is well suited to dairying. The cuisine of the region, and particularly that of northern France, is admired around the world and makes extensive use of milk and milk products.

Several different kinds of adaptation are at work here. Genetic evolution is one component—northern Europe, where dairying is an efficient form of agriculture, gives a reproductive advantage to people with genes for lactose toleration. Technological and economic adaptation made a contribution. The lactose-tolerant population invested in the techniques of dairying, and farmers who adopted and extended these techniques succeeded commercially. Cultural evolution helped complete the picture—the European population, liking dairy products and finding them readily available, created a cuisine that makes good use of them.[4]

Plainly, no one planned the coincidence of a slight difference in genetic composition, a terrain and technology well suited to related agriculture and a culture based around the products of that agriculture. But which of these factors was causal, and which derivative? The answer is both all and none. Genes, technology and society adapted together. Such coevolution—of people and their foodstuffs, of science and technology, of social, political and economic institutions—is the history of economic development.

In business, in politics and in our personal lives, we do not often solve problems directly. The objectives we manage are multiple, incommensurable and partly incompatible. The consequences of what we do depend on responses, both natural and human, that we cannot predict. The systems we try to manage are too complex for us to fully understand. We never have the information about the problem, or the future, we face that we might wish for.

Satisfactory responses in these situations are the result of action, but not the execution of design. These outcomes, achieved obliquely, are the result of iteration and adaptation, experiment and discovery. Reengineering—"'tossing aside old systems and starting over"—is called for only when systems are seriously dysfunctional. And in almost all cases, the best means of reengineering is not "going back to the beginning and inventing a better way of doing work" but trying models that have been successfully tested elsewhere. This is equally true of our personal lives, our corporate organizations and our social and economic structures.

Chapter 17

BEND IT LIKE BECKHAM—
How We Know More Than
We Can Tell

Computers don't solve problems the way people solve problems. Today's computers play chess about as well as humans, but although the formal rules are the same, they are, in a real sense, playing a different game. Computer chess is more direct, grandmaster chess more oblique. People tend to find the grandmaster chess more interesting.

There are no footballing computers. However, footballers don't play football the way computers would play football. David Beckham cannot solve differential equations. He is not only unable to articulate the methods he uses to score goals but apparently ignorant of what they are. Through some oblique process, Beckham has stumbled on the solution to which he would have been led by the—impossible—direct approach, which would have involved a deep understanding of sports engineering and mathematics.

Dr. Carré found this difficult to comprehend (as do I). Yet there is no doubt that Beckham's skills are real.

Few responses seem more direct than the reflex that pulls our hand away from a hot stove. But the process that nature and nurture equipped us with is extraordinarily oblique. We don't pull our hand away because the heat will damage our tissue and our bones. We pull our hand away because it hurts. We probably pull our hand away even before it hurts, because we know that it will hurt. If we know the stove is very hot we will not put our hand on it in the first place.

If we think about it, we recognize that we will suffer serious injury unless we pull our hand away. But we don't actually have that thought, and that isn't why we remove our hand. And yet there is a sense in which it *is* the potential of tissue damage that leads us to pull away. Pain is an evolved capacity that enables humans, and most other creatures, to avoid or reduce damage to their bodies by forcing them to withdraw from threatening situations.

The pain response is sometimes inappropriate. The source of pain may be beneficial—an injection, a lifesaving operation, a visit to the gym. We learn to recognize these anomalies and to develop rules to deal with them: "Accept pain administered by a trusted physician." "No pain no gain" leads you to persist in a workout. But sometimes we need help. Major surgery is possible only because anesthetic drugs interfere with neural responses. These drugs, which dull our reactions, are dangerous. We should not make important decisions under their influence.

If we could master pain reflexes, we could deal directly with decisions about when to pull our hands away from a hot stove and when to allow surgeons to operate on us. We could make decisions on when to risk injury and when not, on the basis of careful calculation and appropriate evidence. Some people make a shot at doing this. Sportsmen and soldiers are trained to ignore pain. They often hurt themselves in consequence. Some people suffer a genetic abnormality in which they do not experience pain, and they generally die young through an accumulation of injuries. Leprosy destroys the nerves that transmit pain, leading to deformity, and historically has been the most feared of all diseases that do not kill.

Scientists have constructed machines that simulate the experience of pain for people who do not experience it naturally. No machine is as sensitive as the natural pain response,[1] but that is not the principal reason pain machines do not work well. They do not work well because patients can switch them off. If you can relieve pain, you will. But the consequence of relieving pain is the damage that results from failure to experience pain. Although there is a great deal of useless pain in the world, on balance we are better off with pain than without it.

Pain is a striking example of an uncalculated reaction that works more effectively than any more considered response. There are many similar examples. Gary Klein has studied over many years the expertise of people like paramedics and firefighters with exceptional practical skills. Just as Kasparov's prowess is evidenced by his victories, and Beckham's by his goals, the expertise of these people is evidenced by their effectiveness and the respect of their colleagues.

One of Klein's experiments involved showing videos of paramedics in action—some novice, some expert—to various

groups of observers. He discovered that both experienced paramedics and laypeople were more successful at distinguishing the
novices from the professionals than were teachers of paramedic
skills.[2] Paramedic teachers monitored adherence to the rules
they taught and saw such adherence more often in the novices.
They looked knowledgeably for directness and could not recognize the success of obliquity from a short video. That doesn't
mean that the teachers were bad teachers or that novice paramedics should not pay close attention to the rules the teachers
prescribe. The key point is that only when you know the rules so
well that they are second nature can you do without them. When
you have learned the direct solution, you begin to learn more
oblique approaches.

The general public, by contrast, didn't know or care
whether the practitioners they observed were following the rules
or not. The qualities the general public tended to value were
confidence and decisiveness—and, most of all, results—and these
were the qualities they generally saw in the most successful paramedics. When Klein interviewed these practitioners, he concluded that pattern recognition rather than calculation was the
key to their success. They used successive limited comparison,
they made an assessment and if evidence seemed inconsistent
with that assessment, they adopted an alternative.

In the same way, novice chess players are taught simple
rules—which exchanges of material should be accepted and
which rejected. Novice chess players often lose because they
make mistakes and don't apply these basic rules. But novices
often lose because they *do* apply these basic rules. A more skillful chess player generally follows the rules but occasionally

breaks them. An entry-level chess computer never makes mistakes in applying the rules but, like a novice chess player, is easy to beat. Practiced obliquity routinely wins against disciplined directness. As it does in the hands of Gary Kasparov. Kasparov is expert not only at applying the rules—he makes few mistakes—but also at understanding when the rules can be broken.

Imbued with the notion that rationality is a process that follows Franklin's rule, we are inclined to think there are some higher-level rules that Beckham, Kasparov and the experienced paramedics are really applying: We just don't know what they are. People spend inordinate amounts of time asking experts like Beckham about the secrets of their success. They don't come away much wiser. There is no reason to think that there is any answer to the implicit question "What set of principles or rules would enable millions of youngsters to bend it like Beckham?"

The same message emerges from the biographies or autobiographies of successful businessmen. They (or at least their ghostwriters) are more articulate than Beckham. But like Beckham, they describe their achievements rather than explain them. More long-windedly, they repeat John Paul Getty's explanation of his business success—"Strike oil." They do not tell us the secret of their achievements because they do not know.

But to say we do not fully understand why people are better than computers at solving so many practical problems or understand why the oblique approach so often outperforms the direct one is not to say we know nothing. Kasparov, Beckham and the paramedics are good at what they do not only because they have exceptional talents but because they have trained and been trained to be good at it over many years.

We often describe our response to pain, or actions such as Beckham's, as intuitive or instinctive. Kasparov's expertise is intellectual, not physical, and it is less likely though not unusual for us to describe his moves as "instinctive" or "intuitive." But these descriptions don't add anything to our knowledge and certainly don't explain why Beckham, who can't do the differential equations, is a better footballer than Dr. Carré, who can. Malcolm Gladwell famously describes the allegedly fake Getty kouros—a Greek statue, expensively purchased and authenticated by careful science, that some art experts immediately perceived as a fake. Gladwell emphasizes the speed of their judgment—*Blink*.[3]

But the speed of expert judgment isn't the main point. The main point is that there is such a thing as expert judgment. If you or I asserted that the kouros was a fake, no one would be very interested. The people who suspected it was a fake were established authorities whose skill and expertise had been developed over many years and who had earned respect for their opinions and judgments in other matters.

These authorities gave partial explanations of what seemed wrong about the statue: Like Kasparov, they are articulate people accustomed to offering explanations for their judgments. They are familiar with Franklin's gambit, and, like Kasparov's explanation of his moves, their accounts are mainly rationalizations of their judgments rather than statements of the process that led to them. "We know more than we can tell," said the polymath Michael Polanyi—certainly more than Beckham can tell, and more even than the highly intelligent Kasparov can tell. We drive our cars successfully even if, like Beckham, we struggle with the differential equations of motion.[4]

The skills of Beckham and Kasparov and the capabilities of the respected art expert are real and verified (as is the expertise of Dr. Carré). If "instinct" leads Beckham to kick winning goals, if "intuitions" enable Kasparov to find the best move or art experts to identify objects as fake, these instincts and intuitions are not voices in the air. They are the expression of finely honed, well-developed skills.

Evolution has given us the pain response because evolution has a better sense of what is good for us than we do ourselves. The calculations are too complex, and we do not know enough about how our bodies work. We lack the information that such calculations would require.

A well-known joke tells of the economist in the wilderness who, when he sees a bear approaching, pulls out his computer and begins to calculate an optimal strategy. His appalled colleague says: "We don't have time for that!" "Don't worry," replies the economist smugly, "the bear has to work out an optimal strategy too." Behind the joke lies a deeply serious point. The bear gains a decisive advantage by not suffering the illusion that the approach based on calculation might work.

Chapter 18

ORDER WITHOUT DESIGN—
How Complex Outcomes
Are Achieved Without Knowledge of
an Overall Purpose

As the economists Ken Arrow and Frank Hahn put it, "The immediate 'common sense' answer to the question 'What will an economy motivated by individual greed and controlled by a very large number of different agents look like?' is probably 'There will be chaos.'"[1] But the outperformance of controlled and planned economies by decentralized, disorganized market systems is perhaps the greatest triumph of obliquity.

An anecdote tells of the Russian planner who visited the United States after the collapse of the Soviet Union. He asked his hosts: "Who is in charge of the supply of bread to New York?" Yet with no one responsible, no directing mind, New York was more reliably supplied with bread than Moscow had been with a planner in charge. The blind watchmaker outperformed the sighted craftsman. The outcome would be hard to believe if it were not our everyday experience.

Not long ago, even people who experienced it did not believe it. Like the bewildered Russians, they found it self-evident that things would work better if someone was in charge. In the 1960s, as the Whiz Kids rose to power in business and politics, there was genuine fear that Russian technological superiority would overtake the West.[2] Only in the 1980s did it become evident how misplaced these fears had been, and only after the fall of the Berlin Wall was it clear just how dismal was the economic performance of the planned economies. Many people who seek to build ever more centralized business organizations, or to institute a global financial architecture, still do not really take the implications of this evidence on board.

The economist Friedrich von Hayek gave a prescient explanation of planning's failures. The evolved complexity that Darwin had observed in nature was also true of economic and social systems. Hayek observed that

> nobody has yet succeeded in deliberately arranging all the activities that go on in a complex society. If anyone did ever succeed in fully organising such a society, it would no longer make use of many minds, but would be altogether dependent on one mind; it would certainly not be very complex but extremely primitive—and so would soon be the mind whose knowledge and will determined everything.[3]

As at the court of Napoleon, in the atelier of Le Corbusier or in the office of Sandy Weill, "there would be none of that interplay of many minds in which alone mind can grow."[4] The achievements of the directing mind would be limited to the knowledge it could absorb and the analysis it could produce.

The product of the watchmaker is limited by his own expertise and skill. Paley's argument that a watch could come into being only by conscious design encounters problems even in its own terms. The watches of his day were the result of centuries of watchmaking tradition. Primitive models were subject to constant modification. A few of these modifications represented improvements and were then incorporated into later generations of watches. No individual watchmaker could build the timepieces on our wrists today.

The complex machinery of the twenty-first century—such as an aircraft—not only incorporates decades of development of aviation technology but is beyond the capacity of any single mind to comprehend. The contributions of many different design teams and the contributions of many different work groups make up the whole.

There is at least in principle a plan of how a 747 works. But you do not start to build a 747 by rolling out such a diagram. Nor would that diagram be of much help if you were asked to fly a 747 or fix one that had gone wrong. For these tasks, you would consult a manual—a simplified account that, like a metaphor or a model, focused on things others had judged you needed to know. Like the London Underground map, any such simplification would be useful for some purposes and not others. The needs of the pilot are very different from those of the maintenance engineer, and they work from different manuals. For any less standard problem it is a matter of judgment what resources are required.

Modern social organization is similarly not the product of any overall conception of what such organization might look like. Adam Smith's colleague Adam Ferguson expressed it clearly: "Nations stumble upon establishments, which are indeed the result of human action, but not the execution of any human design."[5] Even before Darwin, the scholars of the Scottish Enlightenment and thoughtful conservatives such as Edmund Burke had sensed that social organization emerged through iteration and adaptation and was not the product of any serene and lucid mind.

Ferguson was resisting the design theory of Hobbes and Rousseau, who saw political organization as the outcome of an imagined original social contract to which free men might rationally agree. The greatest of the Scottish Enlightenment philosophers, David Hume, was quick to see that Hobbes and Rousseau, like modern social contract theorists such as John Rawls, were engaged in Franklin's gambit: "Each of the factions into which this nation is divided has reared up a fabric of the former kind [a philosophical or speculative system of principles], in order to protect and cover that scheme of actions which it pursues."[6]

Hume understood that the social contract was a metaphor, not a historical description of how government came about. Like all good metaphors and models, it was instructive but not factual. There was no social contract, but the concept of a social contract was a means of emphasizing that legitimate modern government rests on the broad consent of the governed.

And so it is with the closely analogous idea that the modern corporation is a contract between shareholders and managers. The model is a metaphor, not a historical description of how the corporation came into being. As with the social contract metaphor, the perception of corporation as the creation of a contract among its shareholders recognizes that the successful corporation depends on the support of those who own its shares. But anyone who fails to recognize that this is a partial and incomplete description of the nature of the corporation understands little about business reality.

Today, people who deplore the activities of modern business and those who applaud these activities both agree that business is distinguished from other forms of organization by having profit as its defining purpose. Yet this agreement encompasses evident nonsense. Who would want to work for a corporation whose defining purpose was profit, and why would society allow such an organization to exist? People would join that corporation, and society would allow it to function, only if the business met their needs—the needs of the workers for rewarding employment, the needs of the community for goods and services that people want to buy. Needs that change over time and demand that business adapt constantly to meet them. Business exists to serve social purposes and enjoys legitimacy in the short term and survival in the long term only to the extent that business meets these purposes. Profit cannot then be the "defining purpose" of a business.

Yet for years I struggled with the idea that if profit could not be the defining purpose of a corporation, there must be something else that was its defining purpose. If business did not maximize profit, what did it maximize? I was making the same mistake as those victims of the teleological fallacy who struggled for centuries with questions like "What is a tiger for?" Tigers, we now understand, are not the product of any design. Tigers are the creature you would design if you were more skillful and knowledgeable than you could ever be, to do the sorts of things that tigers do. But that is not how they came into existence. Tigers are good at being tigers because adaptation has honed them to be well adapted to the daily life of tigerdom. There is no more, or less, to it than that.

A good oil company is good at being an oil company, just as a good university is good at being a university, a good harpist good at playing the harp or a good dentist good at filling teeth. There is no defining purpose of these activities distinct from the activities themselves. Those who direct businesses must try to balance a multiplicity of objectives and meet the many and incompatible demands that individuals and other organizations make upon them. Any senior manager will tell you this is the reality of how his or her day is spent.

The question that had puzzled me had no answer, and the lack of an answer was not a problem. The people who sought to infer some overall design from the noisy bustle of day-by-day decision making in business were imposing order on confusion, directness on obliquity, like the historians who saw the battle of Borodino as an expression of the will of Napoleon.

Businesses do not maximize anything. The most successful business leaders, such as Marks or Walton or Gates, pursued the unquantifiable but entirely meaningful objective of building a great business. A great business is very good at doing the things we expect a business to do—rewarding its investors, providing satisfying employment, offering goods and services of good quality at reasonable prices, fulfilling a role in the community—and to fail in any of these is, in the long run, to fail in all of them.

To say, as some people do, that doing all these things is really maximizing profit is as confused as the claim that Beckham was really solving some set of complex differential equations. Indeed, to say that successful businesspeople are really maximizing profit is doubly wrong. I know that Beckham scored. I have no idea whether or not Simon Marks maximized profit, and nor did he.

I do know that he built a great business. Marks stumbled on obliquity—and in thinking about his achievement, so did I.

Chapter 19

VERY WELL THEN,
I CONTRADICT MYSELF—
How It Is More Important to Be
Right Than to Be Consistent

Even the most socially inept of economists has noticed that emotions like anger and love play a large role in conventional accounts of human behavior. Some of them also recognize that the happiest people aren't necessarily those who pursue happiness, that the wealthiest people are not the most materialistic, that many of the businesspeople who talk obsessively about profit are ultimately less successful in creating profit than those who profess love for their business.

When happy people talk about their lives, when wealthy people talk about their careers, when the leaders of profitable businesses talk about their companies, they routinely talk about many things besides the pursuit of happiness, wealth or profit: Their accounts of their achievements sound oblique, not direct. But many economists argue that obliquity characterizes only our descriptions, not the underlying substance. In their view, even if our approach seems oblique, the underlying reality is direct. Interpretations of human behavior by the great novelists in terms of the interplay of emotions are mistaken; the oblique accounts that happy people give of their lives, wealthy people give of their motives and the CEOs of successful businesses give of their companies' social responsibility are humbug, or at any rate they differ from the underlying reality.

Of course, we should not rely unconditionally on people's accounts of what they do, so the economists' argument is better than it sounds, though still not a very good one. Its basis is that decisions, especially economic decisions, necessarily involve choices. Even if our objectives are multiple, and unquantifiable, and perhaps ill defined or incommensurable, we still have to make concrete choices. Dame Helen Gardner included some poems in her anthology and left out countless others. Accountants have to report on whether a measure of profit reflects a true and fair view.

If we are consistent in our choices, then we are maximizing our utility—or at least we are maximizing something. This idea, first clearly articulated in Paul Samuelson's *Foundations of Economic Analysis*[1] sixty years ago, rescued economics from a muddle born of nineteenth-century utilitarianism and enabled the subject to become queen of the social sciences. The theory of rational choice dominates economic thinking today, and its influence has spread to politics, psychology and sociology. By denying maximization, we deny rational choice. Obliquity therefore contradicts the theory that has been the most influential doctrine in the social sciences for at least forty years.

Samuelson asserted that consistency was the essence of rationality and that maximization and consistency of choice are in mathematical terms the same thing. If we make a consistent ranking of countries in terms of their human development, we reveal the priorities we attach to the different attributes of human development even if we do not articulate these priorities. If the anthologist is consistent in her choices, some formula like Dr. J. Evans Pritchard's must determine her selection.

Rationality is defined as consistency, and consistency is formally equivalent to maximization. So rational individuals are necessarily engaged in a process of maximization. If there is a flaw in this argument, it must lie in the equation of rationality and consistency. Consistency is not, in fact, an everyday meaning of rationality. Behavior may be consistent but not rational in any ordinary sense of the word. To commune every night with fairies at the bottom of the garden is certainly consistent, but hardly rational. But even if it is possible to be consistent but not rational, surely it is impossible to be rational but not consistent?

I'm not so sure. Suppose I asked you to rank all two hundred countries of the world in terms of the level of human development they had achieved, or to choose the five hundred greatest poems in the English language. If I asked the same question again a month from now, I suspect you would not come up with the same answer. You would rightly be affronted by the suggestion that this was because you were irrational. If I asked you which ranking, which selection, was the correct one, you would say that I was asking a silly question. You had simply chosen to balance incommensurable features in different ways on different occasions. And why not?

Sometimes we want things that are incompatible. We want to eat cream cakes but also to remain slim and fit. We want to give up smoking but we also want another cigarette. We want a secure retirement but we do not want to save. Our expressions of preference often seem contradictory.

Perhaps the preferences we assert—to be fit, to give up smoking, to have a secure old age—are our true preferences. When we eat the cream cake, light a cigarette or spend more when we are young than our financial advisers think we should, we are doing things we don't—really—want to do. Or perhaps what we do reveals our true preferences. The junkie has calculated that the pleasures of successive fixes outweigh the long-run damage to health. People are heroin addicts, or not, because that is what they want.

But these claims about our assertions and our actions are absurd. Many people who want to be slim also want to eat cream cakes, and many smokers really do want to give up. There is nothing irrational about wanting incompatible things. People want to be rich but not to have to work; they want to go to New York but not to have to stand in a security line at the airport. We might think it was irrational not to hold these preferences.

Irrationality does not even lie in resolving incompatible demands in different ways at different times. Visiting a foreign city, you have a recommendation for a local restaurant. You go there, and you like it. You choose fish, and it is excellent—so good that you return the following evening. And now you choose the lamb. Why? Maybe you have acquired new information since

your previous choice. Maybe your tastes have changed. But neither of these explanations is necessary, and neither is probable.
You just chose the fish last night, and the lamb today. That is how
you felt.

The rational-choice theorist might say that you must have
preferred the fish yesterday and the lamb this evening, otherwise you wouldn't have chosen them. Or that you have a taste for
variety. To such a theorist, there is no such thing as obliquity
because, by definition, what we want is whatever is currently the
subject of our direct pursuit.

But these "explanations" of why your behavior is inconsistent are hopeless. Samuelson himself—who was not much
impressed with the extreme versions of his approach adopted
by some of his followers—made the point expressively: "When
the governess of infants caught in a burning building re-enters
it unobserved in a hopeless mission of rescue, casuists may
argue: 'She did it only to get the good feeling of doing it. Because
otherwise she wouldn't have done it'. Such argumentation . . . is
not even wrong."[2]

Rarely in real life are we confronted with—literally—the
same menu of choices. But in the restaurant we are. So were the
two occasions on which we faced the same menu in the same restaurant two identical events on which a rational individual must
make the same choice, or not? To the observer, they appear the
same. To the participant, they may have seemed different. On
what criteria could we resolve the dispute? In a complex and uncertain world, there is no objective basis for deciding whether
what has changed is the options or the choices, the factors that
influence the decision or the decision itself.

In legal proceedings, consistency is of particular importance: We want judges to make predictable decisions and are willing to accept that a consistent decision may be more important than a good one. But outside the legal system the search for precedent as a basis for decision is found only in government bureaucracies and academic life. The process was brilliantly satirized by Francis Cornford, describing the Cambridge University of a century ago (but one that may well be recognized today):

> The *Principle of the Dangerous Precedent* is that you should not now do an admittedly right action for fear you, or your equally timid successors, should not have the courage to do right in some future case, which, *ex hypothesi*, is essentially different, but superficially resembles the present one. Every public action which is not customary, either is wrong, or, if it is right, is a dangerous precedent. It follows that nothing should ever be done for the first time.[3]

The rule of precedent gives considerable scope for Franklin's gambit—for finding formal rationalizations of decisions made on other grounds.

Consistency as a hallmark of rationality belongs to a world far more certain than the one we inhabit. Some people believe there is, in principle, some true and complete description of the world and it is only our perception of the facts, or the accepted consensus about them, that changes. But decisions are being made in light of these properly changing perceptions, and there are no firm criteria that enable us to determine whether two situations are indeed the same or different. What is steadfastness to me may seem dogmatism to you. When you behave consistently, I label you an ideologue; when my behavior is inconsistent, I describe myself as a pragmatist.

In an uncertain environment there can never be any certainty about the nature of the choices we face, and different individuals will perceive the same choices differently. Some people perceive the choices as identical; others do not. What is consistent is subjective, and it is possible to have too much consistency, or too little. Too much consistency is seeing situations as similar when they are in fact different—identifying the specter of Munich with Nasser's seizure of the Suez Canal or Saddam's regime of terror in Iraq. Too little consistency is pragmatism without structure or discipline. The world is too complex and uncertain for consistency to be possible—or even a well-defined concept.

The favorite poet of the Dead Poets Society, Walt Whitman, appreciated the dilemma: "Do I contradict myself? Very well then, I contradict myself. I am large, I contain multitudes."[4] F. Scott Fitzgerald expressed a similar thought: "The test of a first-rate intelligence is the ability to hold two opposed ideas in the mind at the same time and still retain the ability to function."[5] The oblique decision maker, the fox, is not hung up on consistency and frequently holds contradictory ideas simultaneously.

Chapter 20

DODGY DOSSIERS—
How Spurious Rationality Is Often Confused with Good Decision Making

What do people mean when they say it is irrational for us not to play the ultimatum game according to the game theorist's predictions, irrational to reject proposals out of anger or to make them from a sense of fairness? They don't mean that we would be better off if we didn't have these reactions. The neuroscientist Antonio Damasio made famous the case of a patient who, after brain damage, retained his cognitive abilities but operated at a very low level of emotional response. The patient wasn't a better decision maker in consequence: He found it almost impossible to make any decisions at all.[1]

This conception of irrationality doesn't mean that the subjects solve problems badly, just that they don't solve them the way the experimenters think they should. But we get angry, and reject outcomes we think are unfair, for good evolutionary reasons. The authors who wrote that pain was a gift were right, and they might have said the same about love, jealousy, laughter, fairness and justice, hunger, trust, liking and disliking and all the other things that go into our oblique decision making.

Are we better off if we have some control over our anger, our pain, our sense of fairness and unfairness? Certainly. People who get angry all the time find other people unwilling to trade with them, and people who don't get angry at all get trampled on. Complete inability to control the response to pain is damaging, but so is too much control. Even the best calculation we can manage is an imperfect substitute for the evolved response. People who can't control their anger are sociopaths. Those who cannot accept that life is often unfair are rarely happy. But would we be better off if we could switch off our anger or our sense of unfairness? Probably not.

Mostly, we don't have time or ability to calculate the consequences. And if it seemed to our associates that we were making decisions in this calculating way, they would change their behavior toward us. Not necessarily in our favor—but we would have to calculate that too. We do make assessments of how others will behave, how they are likely to react—of course we do. But if our responses are purely calculating, we are not just nasty people but bad decision makers. Like the economist faced with the bear.

Control over our behavior is nevertheless important. Anger was more useful once, when we often wanted people in other tribes to fear us, than it is today.

Our behavior depends not just on what people do but on our beliefs about why they do it and on our familiarity with the wider social context, and for good reasons. That is why "irrational" behavior in the ultimatum game is not irrational at all. We behave fairly if and when we expect other people to behave fairly—and, in the main, not because we have computed the implications. Even if we knew how to do that, we wouldn't have the time, and if we were the kind of people who did compute the implications, we would be different people, and others would react differently toward us.

A satisfying life depends above all on building good personal relationships with other people, but we miss the point if we seek to develop these relationships with our personal happiness as a primary goal. That is why obliquity is fundamental to our dealings with other people. The reactions of others depend not just on what we do but on their beliefs about why we do it—and on their perceptions of the kinds of people we are.

Still, the notion that moral algebra is the best way to decide is deeply ingrained in us, even if we rarely use it when making decisions. So we tell ourselves we are using moral algebra when our real decision processes are oblique—we play Franklin's gambit. Franklin's gambit is perhaps the most common fault in decision making—and particularly in public decision making—today. Politicians and policy makers create an appearance of describing objectives, evaluating options, reviewing evidence. But their descriptions are a sham. The objectives are dictated by the conclusions, the options presented so as to make the favored course look attractive, the data selected to favor the required result. Real alternatives are not assessed rigorously: Policy-based evidence supplants evidence-based policy.

Franklin's gambit—the pretense of following process rationality implied by Franklin's rule—is how we come to have doctored intelligence reports and cost-benefit analyses that are prepared after, not before, the favored policy has been chosen. Franklin's gambit is why we use models in which most of the numbers are made up and that can be reworked to generate any desired outcome. We devote hours to staff evaluations, quality assessments and risk reporting, but these hours are not really devoted to evaluation, assessment or reporting: They are spent ticking boxes. Our personal judgments, our assessments and our risk management are based on other criteria.

When the bus is many minutes behind schedule, you may tell the person who insists on the validity of his model, "That doesn't make sense to me"—you no longer believe the model describes the world. You don't need to have in mind a model that accurately predicts when you should find another means of transport; you only need an accumulation of piecemeal knowledge and experience derived from loosely analogous situations. The dinner guests explained that the Underground map was simply the wrong model for my journey from Paddington to Hyde Park Gardens. But if I had asked, as I might, "When should I use the Underground map?" the only sensible answer would have been "You'll learn as you get to know London better." Judgment and experience teach us which models to use on which occasions.

Obliquity differs from spurious notions of rationality, but it isn't simply decision making by people who have a feel for the situation, an eye for the opportunity, who know in their heart what is right or feel problems in the pit of their stomach. Even when obliquity is not consciously cognitive it is tightly linked to signals in the brain. Good oblique decisions are based on information, analysis and many years of experience, not on what people routinely call "intuition."

Through the intuition that is independent of reason, analysis or specific knowledge, Adolf Hitler apprehended that the world was endangered by a Jewish-Bolshevik conspiracy. He just knew he was right. But he was wrong. Much knowledge is acquired obliquely, and there is much obliquity in the expertise of skilled professionals. But assertions based on such knowledge, or claims to such expertise, are subject to the same tests of empirical validity as other scientific knowledge. The skills of Beckham and Kasparov are proved by their match results, those of firefighters by their success in putting out fires. Gladwell's experts made their judgments after years of training and were respected for their demonstrated expertise.

Pain is a physical reaction to identifiable situations; it has an obvious purpose and physiological origin and is the result of millions of years of evolutionary development. In contrast, the "intuition" that quack medicines cure diseases is worthless, not only because there is no evidence of effectiveness but because it is not possible to explain, even speculatively, how such knowledge might have been acquired. It would be different if the people who had such intuitions had an established record of being proved right in establishing other similar medico-technical relationships.

By lumping a bundle of things together under the headings of instinct and intuition and contrasting them with a particular kind of rationality, by failing to acknowledge the central role that tacit knowledge plays in daily life, we not only fail to see how good judgments are arrived at and good decisions made, but we also open the door to much unscientific nonsense. If we were to insist that Beckham give an account of why he proposed to kick the ball in that particular way before he were allowed to do so, we would quickly lose faith in him. Fortunately, we don't have time. But this demand for explanation is what we do when faced with major decisions in business, politics and finance. Skillful players, who understand the rules of the corporate game even if they don't know how to get the right answer, respond with Franklin's gambit. By downplaying genuine practical knowledge and skill in pursuit of a mistaken notion of rationality we have in practice produced wide irrationality—and many bad decisions.

Conclusions

Chapter 21

THE PRACTICE OF OBLIQUITY—
The Advantages of Oblique
Decision Making

There is a story—perhaps apocryphal—of a professor of decision sciences at a prestigious business school who received
an attractive offer from another highly rated institution. He
sought the advice of a colleague. "You, of all people, are surely
well equipped to make such a decision," said his friend. "Don't
be silly," replied the professor, "this is serious." I suspect Franklin's tongue was in his cheek when he told Priestley how useful
he found moral algebra. He and Darwin (who compiled the pro-
and-con list to help him decide whether to marry) both knew
they didn't really make decisions using Franklin's rule.

But perhaps they thought they should. The success of the
physical sciences has encouraged us to believe there might be a
science of decision making. All kinds of problems in our business and our financial lives, in the political and personal spheres,

could then be managed objectively. Such a scientific procedure would, if done carefully enough, lead every conscientious person to the same answer. As a result, both political and personal disputes could be resolved by applying evidence and rational discourse. The distinction of the great business leader, the measure of financial acumen, would rest only in the ability to arrive at the right answer faster than other people.

There is no such science, and there never will be. Our objectives are typically imprecise and multifaceted; they change as we work toward them, as they should. Our decisions depend on the responses of others and on what we anticipate those responses will be. The world is complex and imperfectly understood, and it always will be.

We do not solve problems in the way the concept of decision science implies, because we can't. The achievement of the great statesman is not to reach the best decision fastest but to mediate effectively among competing views and values. The achievement of the successful business leader is not to foresee the future accurately but to continuously match the capabilities of the firm to the changing market. The test of financial acumen, as described by Buffett and Soros, is to navigate successfully through irresolvable uncertainties.

Mostly, we solve problems obliquely. Our approaches are iterative and adaptive. We make our choices from a limited range of options. Our knowledge of the relevant information, and of what information is relevant, is imperfect. Different people will form different judgments in the same situation, not just because they have different objectives but because they observe different options, select different information and assess that informa-

tion differently; and even with hindsight it will often not be possible to say who was right and who was wrong. In a necessarily
uncertain world, a good decision doesn't necessarily lead to a
good outcome, and a good outcome doesn't necessarily imply
a good decision or a capable decision maker. The notion of a best
solution may itself be misconceived.

The skill of problem solving frequently lies in the interpretation and reinterpretation of high-level objectives. The Japanese approach to Singapore from the landward side was both
direct and oblique, and the eventual attack could then be direct.
The oblique, unaccustomed perspective was how Brunelleschi
cracked the egg, built the dome of Santa Maria del Fiore and discovered how to represent perspective. Many great achievements
are of this kind. Alexander Graham Bell's invention of the tele-
phone, like Akio Morita's creation of the Sony Walkman and
Steve Jobs's reinterpretation of Morita's idea in the iPod, was a
solution to a problem people did not know they had.

It is hard to overstate the damage done recently by people
who thought they knew more about the world than they really
did. The managers and financiers who destroyed great businesses in the unsuccessful pursuit of shareholder value. The
architects and planners who believed that buildings could be
designed from first principles, that vibrant cities could be drawn
on a blank sheet of paper and that expressways should be driven
through the hearts of communities. Acknowledging the complexity of the systems for which they were responsible and the
multiple needs of the individuals who operated these systems
would have avoided these errors.

Such acknowledgment might also have avoided the worst

decisions of the last decade—the Iraq war and the credit expansion of 2003–7. Both these developments were predicated on a knowledge of the world that the decision makers only thought they had. McNamara's description (page 108) of the failure of U.S. policy makers to understand the challenges they faced in Vietnam could be applied to Iraq with only the locations changed. Bank executives believed that their risk-control systems, which they mostly did not understand, enabled them to monitor transactions they also did not understand but believed to be hugely profitable.

Bush and his colleagues were hedgehogs who knew one big thing. Their overriding worldview dictated not only their actions but also their interpretations. The bankers, blinded by greed and trapped by the greed of others, placed private and public reliance on superficial explanations of the profitability and utility of their activities. Neither group saw any reason to ask questions to which they did not wish to hear the answers, and they did not.

The occupants of the Bush White House and the men who played senior roles in great banks also wrongly supposed they had more influence on the world than they did. They imagined they could reconstruct the Middle East on the basis of an American model of lightly regulated capitalism and liberal democracy. They supposed they were in control of large financial institutions, when in fact the floors beneath them were occupied by a rabble of self-interested people determined to evade any controls on their own activities.

What would a politician or banker thinking obliquely have done instead? The answer to that question is to present not an alternative solution but an alternative way of thinking. The alternative to rebuilding Paris to Le Corbusier's crazed design was not to rebuild Paris according to some other grand design but rather to grasp that Paris would develop, as it had for centuries, through a process of constant adaptation. Most construction survives at most a few generations, but Notre Dame, two centuries in the building, remains magnificent seven hundred years later. The Eiffel Tower, intended as a temporary structure, has been the city's most distinctive landmark for over a century. The Gare d'Orsay, which ceased to be a train station, has regained relevance as the Musée d'Orsay. London grew by muddling through, Brasilia by design; London is a great city; Brasilia is not.

The direct approach to problem solving requires us to know the method of solution before we start. Even if such a method is possible, it is often inefficient—the computer solves the sudoku problem, but in a laborious way. Iteration and experience lead us to the best principles of analysis. In obliquity, we learn about the structure of a problem as we solve it. Klein's paramedics and firefighters became competent by learning the rules and became good through practice.

When faced with a task that daunts you, a project that you find difficult, begin by doing *something*. Choose a small component that seems potentially relevant to the task. While it seems sensible to plan everything before you start, mostly you can't: Objectives are not clearly enough defined, the nature of the problem keeps shifting, it is too complex and you lack sufficient information. The direct approach is simply impossible. Every writer has stared at a blank page, waiting for inspiration. The wait is often lengthy. Get it down. That is how this book was written, and it couldn't have been done in any other way. Only an oblique approach could have worked.

The foresters of the National Park Service learned how to manage their forest through trial and error. But that trial and error was not a random process. The foresters learned through a process of adaptation, aided by simulations from computer modeling. They used these models, as any such models should be used, not to make decisions or to predict the future but to understand better the complex systems they were dealing with. The models aided the practiced judgment of foresters but did not replace it.

Good decision making is pragmatic and eclectic. Oblique approaches rely on a tool kit of models and narratives rather than any simple or single account. To fit the world into a single model or narrative fails to acknowledge the universality of uncertainty and complexity.

The reputation of financial economics has never recovered from the blow of the virtual collapse of Long-Term Capital Management, a sophisticated practitioner of the risk models outlined in chapter twelve, and the involvement of two Nobel Prize winners, Robert C. Merton and Myron Scholes. The fund built huge positions on the basis of estimated mispricings, relying on its models to control its exposures. When the Asian financial crisis blew up in 1997, the fund managers extended their positions. They believed their own models. Their failure was a precursor of the much larger failures that would follow a decade or so later.

At the banks a decade later, as in Iraq, evidence and models were used to confirm what was already asserted to be true rather than to challenge the validity of prior assumptions. And in both cases a superficial appearance of considered rationality concealed the crude directness of what was really being done.

Oblique problem solving is not less rational than Franklin's rule but more so. Obliquity doesn't mean that we should stop thinking about objectives, fail to examine options or omit to seek information and understand as best we can the complex systems that we deal with. The alternative to a "rational" process of defining objectives, evaluating options, modeling consequences is an oblique approach that is truly based on reason and evidence.

When Beckham scored that famous goal, when experts concluded the Getty kouros was a fake, when Picasso drew a cockerel with a few brushstrokes, these were all the considered moves of highly trained and skilled professionals. These people knew what they were doing, even if none of them could explain very well why they did it or how it contributed to their high-level goals. In retrospect, of course, we understand better what they did (and so might they). To call these processes intuition is to miss the central point, which is that what we are describing as intuition is based on evidence and evaluation and is repeatedly successful when practiced by a Beckham, an experienced art curator or a Picasso—and not successful at the feet, or in the hands or minds, of amateur footballers, casual gallery visitors or weekend artists. The more we practice the better our judgments.

I struggled to form a personal view in the run-up to the invasion of Iraq. The issues seemed to me too wide, the implications so extensive, the information available so limited. With hindsight, I believe the right way to have formed an opinion would have been to say: "I do not trust the judgment of the people who are making this decision or their ability to handle the consequences." That would have led to the right conclusion, and for the right reasons.

There is nothing wrong with using trust as a basis for decision. Finding people you can trust, or establishing trusting relationships with them, is the most effective—often the only effective—means of achieving the delegation that is necessary to accomplish objectives and goals in large organizations. Successful decentralization relies on the transmission of high-level objectives, not just intermediate goals and basic actions, to the agents who will implement them. This is a world apart from principal-agent models that treat social organizations as mechanical systems in which agents respond to the stimuli that incentive structures impose.

If you are clear about your high-level goals and knowledgeable enough about the systems their achievement depends on, then you can solve problems in a direct way. But goals are often vague, interactions unpredictable, complexity extensive, problem descriptions incomplete, the environment uncertain. That is where obliquity comes into play.

There is nothing wrong with anger, or a sense of fairness, or jealousy, or love, as motives for decisions, and we need not be apologetic about them. Such feelings convey relevant information, and it would be as much a mistake to disregard them as to make them the sole basis of decision. Just as it would be a mistake to treat a model, or Franklin's list of pros and cons, as the sole basis of decision. Good decision making is oblique because it is iterative and experimental: It constantly adapts as new information, of many kinds, becomes available. Much of that information comes from the process of decision making itself.

Only an arrogant man would believe he could plan a city; only an unimaginative man would want to. The men who launched the Iraq war, the bankers responsible for the credit crunch, were both arrogant and unimaginative. Clever, and more imaginative, people—like Brunelleschi when he discovered perspective and constructed the dome of Santa Maria del Fiore or Wiles when he solved Fermat's last theorem—sometimes find direct solutions, but that is because they understand clearly the problems to which direct solutions may apply.

Obliquity is the best approach whenever complex systems evolve in an uncertain environment and whenever the effect of our actions depends on the ways in which others respond to them. There is a role for carrots and sticks, but to rely on carrots and sticks alone is effective only when we employ donkeys and we are sure exactly what we want the donkeys to do. Directness is only appropriate when the environment is stable, objectives are one-dimensional and transparent and it is possible to determine when and whether goals have been achieved. The world of politics and business today is afflicted by many hedgehogs, men and women who mistakenly believe the world is like that.

Acknowledgments

This book originates in an article titled "Obliquity" that appeared in the *Financial Times* weekend magazine on January 17, 2004. Daniel Crewe of Profile Books urged me to develop the argument into a book, and his persistence and helpful editing led to the present volume. Eamon Dolan of Penguin Press did far more than translate pounds into dollars, enabling me to clarify the thesis at many points. The genesis of the ideas is derived from a series of discussions with Jeremy Hardie in 2002–3, and I am grateful to him and to Adam Ridley, Mervyn King and Ed Smith for their comments on a draft of the manuscript. Johanna De Santis provided efficient and meticulous research assistance and Jo Charrington managed the writing process from first draft to final product. I am very grateful to all of them.

Notes

Preface

1. Benjamin Franklin, *The Autobiography of Benjamin Franklin* (1791; reprint, New Haven, CT: Yale University Press, 1964), p. 88.
2. Dan Ariely, *Predictably Irrational* (London: Harper Collins, 2008).

Chapter 1: Obliquity—Why Our Objectives Are Often Best Pursued Indirectly

1. John Stuart Mill, *Autobiography* (1873; reprint, London: Penguin, 1989), p. 117.
2. Jim Collins and Jerry I. Porras, *Built to Last: Successful Habits of Visionary Companies* (London: Random House Business Books, 2000), p. 8.
3. Adam Smith, *An Inquiry into the Nature and Causes of the Wealth of Nations* (1776; abridged with commentary, Indianapolis and Cambridge: Hackett, 1993), p. 130.
4. Emily Dickinson, *Emily Dickinson*, ed. L. Dickey (New York: Dell, 1960), p. 107.
5. John Keats, "On First Looking into Chapman's Homer," in *Poems by John Keats* (London: Methuen, n.d.).
6. Richard Weston, *Modernism* (London: Phaidon Press, 1996).
7. Charles Jencks, *The Language of Post-Modern Architecture* (London, Academy Editions, 1984), p. 9.
8. Le Corbusier, *Toward a New Architecture* (London, Architectural Press, 1982), p. 10.
9. Marseille's Unité d'Habitation, also known as La Cité Radieuse, was built in 1947–52 and combined Le Corbusier's vision of communal living with the needs of postwar France for social housing.
10. Michael Hammer and James Champy, *Reengineering the Corporation: A Manifesto for Business Revolution* (London: Nicholas Brearley, 1995), p. 31.
11. Vladimir Ilyich Lenin, *Essential Works of Lenin: "What Is to Be Done?"* (1902; reprint, New York: Dover, 1987).
12. Le Corbusier, *The Radiant City* (London: Faber & Faber, 1964), p. 154.

Chapter 2: Fulfillment—How the Happiest People Do Not Pursue Happiness

1. Reinhold Messner, *The Crystal Horizon: Everest: The First Solo Ascent* (Ramsbury, UK: Crowood Press, 1989), p. 244.

2. *New York Times*, "Climbing Mount Everest Is Work of Supermen," March 18, 1923.

3. Mihalyi Csikszentmihalyi, *Living Well* (London: Weidenfeld & Nicolson, 1997), pp. 28–9.

4. For surveys of evidence on sources of happiness, see, e.g., Daniel Nettle, *Happiness— The Science Behind Your Smile* (Oxford: Oxford University Press, 2005); Richard Layard, *Happiness: Lessons from a New Science* (London: Allen Lane, 2005); David G. Myers, *The Pursuit of Happiness: Who Is Happy and Why?* (London: Aquarian Press, 1993); Jonathan Haidt, *The Happiness Hypothesis* (London: Arrow Books, 2006).

5. Mihalyi Csikszentmihalyi, *Flow: The Psychology of Optimal Experience* (New York: Harper Perennial, 1990); Nettle, *Happiness*.

6. Aldous Huxley, *Brave New World* (London: Chatto and Windus, 1932).

7. Robert Nozick, *Anarchy, State and Utopia* (Oxford: Blackwell, 1995), pp. 42–5.

8. Oscar Wilde, *The Picture of Dorian Gray* (1890; reprint, Mineola, NY: Dover Publications, 1993), p. 79.

9. *The Pursuit of Happyness*, directed by Gabriele Muccino (Columbia Pictures, 2006).

10. Chris Gardner with Quincy Troupe, *The Pursuit of Happyness* (New York: Amistad, 2006).

11. Nettle, *Happiness*; Layard, *Happiness*.

Chapter 3: The Profit-Seeking Paradox—How the Most Profitable Companies Are Not the Most Profit Oriented

1. ICI, "Annual Report," 1990.

2. ICI, "Annual Report," 1997.

3. Jim Collins and Jerry I. Porras, *Built to Last: Successful Habits of Visionary Companies* (London: Random House Business Books, 2000), p. 81.

4. Ibid., p. 81.

5. Quoted in Will Hutton, *The World We're In* (London: Little, Brown, 2002), p. 131.

6. *BusinessWeek*, April 7, 1998, quoted in Hutton, *The World We're In*.

7. *Washington Post*, November 16, 2004.

8. George Merck II, speech to Medical College of Virginia, December 1, 1950, quoted in Collins and Porras, *Built to Last*, p. 48.

9. *Forbes*, December 15, 1962, quoted in Collins and Porras, *Built to Last*, p. 49.

10. Jim Collins, *How the Mighty Fall* (London: Random House Business Books, 2009), p. 50.

11. *Fortune International*, "Top 100 Most Admired Companies," various years.

12. Robert Johnson in 1943. See http://www.jnj.com/connect/about-jnj/jnj-credo.

13. Aiko Morita, *Made in Japan* (London: Collins, 1987), pp. 147–8.

14. Monica Langley, *Tearing Down the Walls* (New York: Simon & Schuster, 2003), pp. 324–5.

15. Ibid.

16. M. Nakamoto and D. Wighton, "Citigroup Chief Stays Bullish on Buy-outs," *Financial Times*, July 10, 2007.

17. John Horton and Susan Mendus, *After MacIntyre: Critical Perspectives on the Work of Alasdair MacIntyre* (Cambridge: Polity, 1994), p. 285.

18. C. R. Christensen, J. W. Rosenblum, and C. B. Weigle, "Prelude Corporation," *Harvard Business School Case Studies*, August 1, 1972.

19. Horton and Mendus, *After MacIntyre*, p. 285.

20. F. Guerrera, "Welch Condemns Share Price Focus," *Financial Times*, March 13, 2009.

21. Jack Welch, "Jack Welch Elaborates: Shareholder Value," *BusinessWeek*, March 16, 2009.

Chapter 4: The Art of the Deal—How the Wealthiest People Are Not the Most Materialistic

1. Ron Chernow, *Titan: The Life of John D. Rockefeller, Sr.* (London: Little, Brown, 1998), p. 153.

2. Andrew Carnegie, *The Gospel of Wealth and Other Timely Essays* (1889), ed. E. C. Kirkland (Cambridge, MA: Belknap Press,1962), p. 29.

3. Sam Walton with John Huey, *Made in America: My Story* (New York, Bantam, 1993), p. 298.

4. Donald J. Trump with Tony Schwartz, *Trump: The Art of the Deal* (New York, Warner Books, 1987), p. 1.

5. John Stuart Mill, *Autobiography* (1873; reprint, London: Penguin, 1989), p. 117.

6. Richard Conniff, *The Natural History of the Rich* (New York: Norton, 2002), p. 102.

7. Boyden Sparkes and Samuel Taylor Moore, *Hetty Green: A Woman Who Loved Money* (London: William Heinemann, 1930).

8. Aristotle, *The Politics* (London: Penguin, 1992) book I, chapter XI.

9. Albert J. Dunlap with Bob Andelman, *Mean Business: How I Save Bad Companies and Make Good Companies Great* (New York: Fireside, 1996), p. xii.

10. Securities and Exchange Commission, "Enforcement Proceedings," *SEC News Digest* 2002-171, September 4, 2002.

11. Quoted in James B. Stewart, *Den of Thieves* (New York: Simon & Schuster, 1991), p. 223.

12. Michael Lewis, *Liar's Poker: Two Cities, True Greed* (London: Hodder & Stoughton, 1989).

13. Connie Bruck, *The Predators' Ball: The Inside Story of Drexel Burnham and the Rise of the Junk Bond Raider* (London: Penguin, 1989).

14. House Committee on Oversight and Government Reform, Transcript of Hearing (Richard Fuld), October 6, 2008.

15. Ken Auletta, *Greed and Glory on Wall Street: The Fall of the House of Lehman* (Harmondsworth, UK: Penguin, 1986), p. 235.

16. Lehman was at that time rescued by American Express, which floated the firm in 1994 ahead of its final collapse in 2008.

Chapter 5: Objectives, Goals and Actions—How the Means Help Us Discover the End

1. Plutarch, *Plutarch's Lives* (London, William Heinemann, 1948), p. 483.

2. Daniel Nettle, *Happiness: The Science Behind Your Smile* (Oxford: Oxford University Press, 2005), p. 18.

3. See, for example, C. D. Ryff, "Happiness Is Everything, or Is It?" *Journal of Personality and Social Psychology* 57, no. 6 (1989); Daniel Kahneman, "Objective Happiness," in Daniel Kahneman, Ed Diener, and Norbert Schwarz, *Well-being: The Foundations of Hedonic Psychology* (New York, Russell Sage Foundation, 2001).

4. Jack Welch, "Jack Welch Elaborates: Shareholder Value," *BusinessWeek*, March 16, 2009.

5. Ed Smith, *What Sport Tells Us About Life* (London: Penguin, 2008), p. 28.

6. Bob Rotella with Bob Cullen, *Golf Is Not a Game of Perfect* (London: Pocket Books, 2004).

Chapter 6: The Ubiquity of Obliquity—How Obliquity Is Relevant to Many Aspects of Our Lives

1. Giorgio Vasari, *Lives of the Painters, Sculptors, and Architects* (London, George Bell & Sons, 1878), vol. I, p. 431.

2. Ernst H. Gombrich, *The Story of Art* (Oxford, Phaidon Press, 1978), p. 8.

3. Pablo Picasso to Marius de Zaya in *Arts*, May 1923, reproduced in Alfred H. Barr, *Picasso: Fifty Years of His Art* (New York, Museum of Modern Art, 1946), p. 270.

4. Simon Singh, *Fermat's Last Theorem* (London, Fourth Estate, 1997).

5. U.S. National Park Service, "The Yellowstone Fires of 1988," 2008.

6. B. M. Kilgore, "Origin and History of Wildland Fire Use in the U.S. National Park System," *George Wright Forum* 24, no. 3 (2007).

7. Le Corbusier, *The Radiant City* (London, Faber & Faber, 1964), p.154.

8. Robert A. Caro, *The Power Broker: Robert Moses and the Fall of New York* (New York, Vintage Books, 1975), p. 11.

9. Jane Jacobs, *The Death and Life of Great American Cities* (Harmondsworth, UK: Penguin, 1965), p. 350.

10. Louis Pasteur, 1854, quoted in Maurice B. Strauss, *Familiar Medical Quotations* (London: J & A Churchill, 1968), p. 108.

Chapter 7: Muddling Through—Why Oblique Approaches Succeed

1. Charles Lindblom, "The Science of "Muddling Through," *Public Administration Review* 19, no. 2 (1959), pp. 79–88.

2. H. Igor Ansoff, *Corporate Strategy* (Harmondsworth, UK: Penguin, 1985), p. 41.

3. Ibid., p. 10.

4. Ibid., p. 312.

5. Robert Heller in Ansoff, *Corporate Strategy*, p. 360.

6. Ansoff, *Corporate Strategy*, pp. 326–7.

7. Saint-Gobain, "Annual Report 2008," Courbevoie, 2008.

8. Charles Lindblom, "Still Muddling, Not Yet Through," *Public Administration Review* 39, no. 6 (1979), pp. 517–26.

9. Cass R. Sunstein, *Legal Reasoning and Political Conflict* (Oxford: Oxford University Press, 1996), chapter 2.

Chapter 8: Pluralism—Why There Is Usually More Than One Answer to a Problem

1. *Dead Poets Society*, directed by Peter Weir (Touchstone Pictures, 1989).

2. Dr. H. Igor Ansoff was a real person—he died in 2002. Dr. J. Evans Pritchard is not.

3. Helen Gardner, ed., *The New Oxford Book of English Verse, 1250–1950* (Oxford: Oxford University Press, 1972).

4. HM Treasury, *Microeconomic Reform in Britain: Delivering Opportunities for All*, ed. E. Balls, G. O'Donnell, and J. Grice (Houndmills, UK: Palgrave Macmillan, 2004).

5. "I often say that when you can measure what you are speaking about, and express it

in numbers, you know something about it; but when you cannot measure it, when you cannot express it in numbers, your knowledge is of a meagre and unsatisfactory kind." Lord Kelvin's lecture on "Electrical Units of Measurement," 1883, reproduced in *Popular Lectures and Addresses* (London: Macmillan, 1891) vol. 1, p. 73.

6. United Nations Development Programme, *Human Development Report* (New York: Palgrave Macmillan, various years). Available at http://hdr.undp.org.

7. Derived from the United Nations Human Development Index Web site.

   L is life expectancy at birth.

   R is adult literacy rate (percent).

   E is gross enrollment index (combined primary, secondary and tertiary gross enrollment).

   G is GDP per capita at purchasing power parity.

8. Aristotle, *Nicomachean Ethics* (Cambridge: Cambridge University Press, 2000), 1, 4.

9. J. A. Kay, Jeremy Edwards, and Colin P. Mayer, *The Economic Analysis of Accounting Profitability* (Oxford: Oxford University Press, 1987).

10. Isaiah Berlin, I., *Four Essays on Liberty* (London: Oxford University Press, 1969) and Isaiah Berlin, "My Intellectual Path," *New York Review of Books* XLV, no. 8 (1998).

11. Berlin, *Four Essays on Liberty*.

12. Gardner, *New Oxford Book of English Verse*, p. v.

13. Jonathan Lopez, *The Man Who Made Vermeers: Unvarnishing the Legend of Master Forger Han van Meegeren* (New York: Mariner Books, 2008).

14. Matthew Cullerne Brown, *Art Under Stalin* (Oxford: Phaidon Press, 1991); Berthold Hinz, *Art in the Third Reich* (Oxford: Blackwell, 1980).

Chapter 9: Interaction—Why the Outcome of What We Do Depends on How We Do It

1. Judi Bevan, *The Rise and Fall of Marks and Spencer: And How it Rose Again* (London: Profile Books, 2001), p. 33; Israel M. Sieff, *Memoirs* (London: Weidenfeld & Nicolson, 1970), pp. 157–8.

2. In 1998, Marks & Spencer reported record margins and profits in excess of one billion pounds for the first—and only—time. Within a few months, sales and profits had fallen. In the following decade the company has experienced repeated business reorganization and takeover rumors. (See Marks & Spencer, "Annual Report," 1998.)

3. Elizabeth Jane Whately, *Life and Correspondence of Richard Whately, D.D.* (London: Longmans, Green, 1866), vol. II, p. 402.

4. R. F. Foster, *Modern Ireland* (London: Penguin, 1989) and R. F. Foster, *The Irish Story: Telling Tales and Making It Up in Ireland* (London: Allen Lane, 2001).

5. Michael Blastland and Andrew Dilnot, *The Tiger That Isn't: Seeing Through a World of Numbers* (London: Profile, 2007), pp. 76–7.

6. C. A. E. Goodhart, "Monetary Relationships: A View from Threadneedle Street," Reserve Bank of Australia, *Papers in Monetary Economics* 1 (1975).

Chapter 10: Complexity—How the World Is Too Complex for Directness to Be Direct

1. H. A. Simon and A. Newell, "Heuristic Problem Solving: The Next Advance in Operations Research," *Operations Research* 6, no. 1 (Jan.–Feb. 1958), pp.1–10.

2. Hubert L. Dreyfus, *What Computers Still Can't Do* (Cambridge, MA: MIT Press, 1992), p. 80.

3. Benjamin Franklin to Joseph Priestley, 1772, in Ronald W. Clark, *Benjamin Franklin: A Biography* (London: Weidenfeld & Nicolson, 1983), pp. 363–4.

4. Charles Darwin, *The Autobiography of Charles Darwin*, ed. N. Barlow (London: Collins, 1958), pp. 231–3.

5. Benjamin Franklin, *The Autobiography of Benjamin Franklin* (1791; reprint, New Haven, CT: Yale University Press, 1964), p. 88.

6. John A. Byrne, *The Whiz Kids: The Founding Fathers of American Business—and the Legacy They Left Us* (New York: Bantam Doubleday Dell, 1993).

7. David Halberstam, *The Reckoning* (London: Bloomsbury, 1987), p. 201.

8. Spencer C. Tucker, ed., *Encyclopedia of the Vietnam War* (Santa Barbara, CA: ABC-CLIO, 1998).

9. Kenneth Spencer, quoted in Byrne, *Whiz Kids*, p. 420.

10. Robert Sobel, *The Rise and Fall of the Conglomerate Kings* (New York: Stein and Day, 1984), p. 47.

11. R. T. Pascale, "Perspectives on Strategy: The Real Story Behind Honda's Success," *California Management Review* 26, no. 3 (1984), p. 47.

12. Ibid.

13. Robert S. McNamara with Brian VanDeMark, *In Retrospect: The Tragedy and Lessons of Vietnam* (New York: Vintage, 1996), pp. 321 and 339.

Chapter 11: Incompleteness—How We Rarely Know Enough About the Nature of Our Problems

1. Arthur Quiller-Couch, ed., *Oxford Book of English Verse 1250–1918* (1919; reprint, Oxford: Clarendon Press, 1961).

2. Christopher Ricks, ed., *The Oxford Book of English Verse* (Oxford: Oxford University Press, 1999).

3. Theodore Levitt, "Marketing Myopia," *Harvard Business Review* 38, no. 4 (Jul.–Aug. 1960), pp. 45–56.

4. Carl W. Stern and George Stalk, eds., *Perspectives on Strategy from the Boston Consulting Group* (New York: John Wiley, 1998).

5. For similar illusions, see http://www.planetperplex.com/en/item131.

Chapter 12: Abstraction—Why Models Are Imperfect Descriptions of Reality

1. Jorge Luis Borges, *A Universal History of Infamy* (Harmondsworth, UK: Penguin, 1975), p. 131.

2. Value at risk is a group of related models that compute the maximum potential change in value of a portfolio of assets under "normal" market conditions. (See also: JPMorgan and Reuters, *RiskMetrics—Technical Document*, 4th ed. (New York: Morgan Guaranty Trust Company of New York, 1996); Joe Nocera, "Risk Management," *New York Times*, January 4, 2009.)

3. Bruce Pandolfini, *Kasparov and Deep Blue: The Historic Chess Match Between Man and Machine* (New York: Simon & Schuster, 1997).

4. David G. Stork, ed., *Hal's Legacy: 2001's Computer as a Dream and Reality* (Cambridge, MA, MIT, 1997), chapter 5.

5. J. Gale, K. G. Binmore, and L. Samuelson, "Learning to Be Imperfect: The Ultimatum Game," *Games and Economic Behavior* 8, no. 1 (1995), pp. 56–90.

Chapter 13: The Flickering Lamp of History—How We Mistakenly Infer Design from Outcome

1. M. Meyer, "From a Champ to a Chump," *Newsweek*, July 26, 1993.
2. Alasdair MacIntyre, *After Virtue: A Study in Moral Theory*, 2nd edition (London, Gerald Duckworth, 1994), p. 75.
3. Leo Tolstoy, *War and Peace* (1869; reprint, Ware, UK: Wordsworth Editions, 1993), book X, chapters 27 and 28.
4. M. Carré, T. Asai, T. Akatsuka, and S. J. Haake, "The Curve Kick of a Football I: Impact with the Foot," *Sports Engineering* 5, no. 4 (2002); M. Carré, T. Asai, T. Akatsuka, and S. J. Haake, "The Curve Kick of a Football II: Flight Through the Air," *Sports Engineering* 5, no. 4 (2002).
5. See, for example, T. Gilovich, R. Vallone, and A. Tversky, "The Hot Hand in Basketball: On the Misperception of Random Sequences," *Cognitive Psychology*, vol. 17 (1985); A. Wilke and H. C. Barrett, "The Hot Hand Phenomenon as a Cognitive Adaptation to Clumped Resources," *Evolution and Human Behavior* 30, no. 3 (2009); M. Bar-Eli, S. Avugosa, and M. Raab, "Twenty Years of 'Hot Hand' Research: Review and Critique," *Psychology of Sport and Exercise* 7, no. 6 (2006).
6. Nassim Nicholas Taleb, *Fooled by Randomness* (New York: Texere, 2001).
7. Tolstoy *War and Peace*, book X, chapters 27 and 28.
8. M. Kets de Vries, "Leaders Who Make a Difference," *European Management Journal* 14, no. 5 (October 1996), pp. 486–93.
9. Philip M. Rosenzweig, *The Halo Effect* (New York: Free Press, 2007), p. 107.
10. Ibid.; Philip M. Rosenzweig, "What Do We Think Happened at ABB? Pitfalls in Research About Firm Performance," *International Journal of Management and Decision Making* 5, no. 4 (2004); D. Bilefsky and A. Raghavan, "How ABB Tumbled Back Down to Earth," *Wall Street Journal* (Europe), January 23, 2003.
11. Neville Chamberlain, "Peace in Our Time," speech to House of Commons, September 30, 1938.
12. Winston Churchill, "Upon the Death of Neville Chamberlain," speech to House of Commons, November 12, 1940.

Chapter 14: The Stockdale Paradox—How We Have Less Freedom of Choice Than We Think

1. Jim Collins, *Good to Great* (London: Random House Business Books, 2001), p. 83.
2. Roy Jenkins, *Churchill* (London: Macmillan, 2001), p. 613.
3. Robert A. Caro, *The Years of Lyndon Johnson* (London: Bodley Head, 1990).
4. Franklin Delano Roosevelt, *Looking Forward* (London: William Heinemann, 1933), p. 51.

Chapter 15: The Hedgehog and the Fox—How Good Decision Makers Recognize the Limits of Their Knowledge

1. Lawrence A. Cunningham, *The Essays of Warren Buffett: Lessons for Investors and Managers* (Singapore: John Wiley & Sons, 2002), p. 124.

2. George Soros, *The Alchemy of Finance* (Hoboken, NJ: John Wiley & Sons, 2003), p. 309.

3. Isaiah Berlin, *The Fox and the Hedgehog: An Essay on Tolstoy's View of History* (London: Weidenfeld & Nicolson, 1953).

4. Philip E. Tetlock, *Expert Political Judgment: How Good Is It? How Can We Know?* (Princeton, NJ: Princeton University Press, 2005), pp. 72–86.

5. John Maynard Keynes, *The Collected Writings of John Maynard Keynes*, vol. X (London: Macmillan Press, 1972), vol. X, p. 186.

6. Joseph Conrad, *Typhoon and Other Stories* (London: William Heinemann, 1903), chapter 2.

7. Ibid.

Chapter 16: The Blind Watchmaker—How Adaptation Is Smarter Than We Are

1. William Paley, *Natural Theology* (1802; reprint, Weybridge, UK: Hamilton, n.d.), chapter 1.

2. Richard Dawkins, *The Blind Watchmaker* (Harlow, UK: Longman Scientific & Technical, 1986).

3. Richard Dawkins, *The Selfish Gene* (Oxford: Oxford University Press, 1989).

4. William H. Durham, *Coevolution: Genes, Culture, and Human Diversity* (Stanford, CA: Stanford University Press, 1991), chapter 5.

Chapter 17: Bend It Like Beckham—How We Know More Than We Can Tell

1. Paul Brand and Philip Yancey, *The Gift of Pain: Why We Hurt and What We Can Do About It* (Grand Rapids, MI: Zondervan, 1997), p. 91.

2. Gary A. Klein, *Sources of Power: How People Make Decisions* (Cambridge, MA: MIT Press, 1998), p. 150.

3. Malcolm Gladwell, *Blink* (London: Allen Lane, 2005), pp. 3–8.

4. Michael Polanyi, *The Tacit Dimension* (Gloucester, MA: Peter Smith, 1983), p. 4.

Chapter 18: Order Without Design—How Complex Outcomes Are Achieved Without Knowledge of an Overall Purpose

1. Kenneth J. Arrow and F. H. Hahn, *General Competitive Analysis* (Amsterdam: North Holland, 1971), p. vii.

2. John A. Byrne, *The Whiz Kids: The Founding Fathers of American Business—and the Legacy They Left Us* (New York: Bantam Doubleday Dell, 1993).

3. Friedrich von Hayek, *Law, Legislation and Liberty*, (Chicago: University of Chicago Press, 1973), vol. 1, "Rules and Order," p. 49.

4. Ibid.

5. Adam Ferguson, *An Essay on the History of Civil Society* (1767; reprint, Edinburgh: Edinburgh University Press, 1966), p. 122.

6. David Hume, *Essays: Moral, Political, Literary* (1777; reprint, ed. Eugene F. Miller, Indianapolis: Liberty Classics, 1985), book II, chapter XII.

Chapter 19: Very Well Then, I Contradict Myself—How It Is More Important to Be Right Than to Be Consistent

1. Paul Samuelson, *Foundations of Economic Analysis* (1947; reprint, Cambridge, MA: Harvard University Press, 1966).

2. Paul Samuelson, "Altruism as a Problem Involving Group Versus Individual Selection in Economics and Biology," *American Economic Review* 83, no. 2 (May 1998), pp. 143–8.

3. Francis M. Cornford, *Microcosmographia Academica* (Cambridge: Bowes & Bowes, 1908), chapter VII.

4. Walt Whitman, "Song of Myself," in *Leaves of Grass* (1855; reprint, Hertfordshire, UK: Wordsworth Editions, 2006), p. 69.

5. F. Scott Fitzgerald, "The Crack-up," *Esquire*, February 1936.

Chapter 20: Dodgy Dossiers—How Spurious Rationality Is Often Confused with Good Decision Making

1. Antonio Damasio, *Descartes' Error: Emotion, Reason, and the Human Brain* (New York: Quill, 2000).

Bibliography

I should give credit to the people whose insights have led me to think about obliquity and its implications for our business, political and personal lives. I am indebted to Robert Solomon, whose admirable *Ethics and Excellence* relieved me of the burden of the economist's credo that everyone must be maximizing something and introduced me to the notion that Aristotle might have had something to say about a commercial world he could not have imagined. Indebted too to the leading modern proponent of virtue ethics, Alasdair MacIntyre, who imagined it only with revulsion. James Scott's superb *Seeing Like a State* is a fertile source of both ideas and examples of the failure of directness and modernism in economic affairs, and I have borrowed both the ideas and the examples shamelessly.

The maxim "We know more than we can tell," which is fundamental to obliquity, encapsulates Michael Polanyi's exposition of tacit knowledge, an idea that many have had but few have so well expressed. Richard Sennett's *The Craftsman* has recently provided an elegant exposition of related theories.

Matt Ridley's *Origins of Virtue* introduced me to the idea that many of our social and economic institutions can best be explained with the aid of evolutionary psychology; in a very different style, Ken Binmore and Herbert Gintis explore similar themes. And the attack on Franklin's rule as the epitome of rational thought comes today from many quarters, especially the projects on decision making led by Gerd Gigerenzer. Behavioral economics tends, as I have described, to persist in the notion that the failure of standard concepts of rationality is a problem in our own behavior rather than in our models, but the work of Dan Kahneman and Amos Tversky must nevertheless be credited with a transformation in the way I—and many others—think about economic behavior.

Ansoff, H. Igor. *Corporate Strategy*. Harmondsworth, UK: Penguin, 1985.

Ariely, Dan. *Predictably Irrational*. London: HarperCollins, 2008.

Aristotle. *Nicomachean Ethics*. Cambridge: Cambridge University Press, 2000.

Aristotle. *The Politics*. London: Penguin, 1992.

Arrow, Kenneth J., and F. H. Hahn. *General Competitive Analysis*. Amsterdam: North Holland Publishing, 1971.

Auletta, Ken. *Greed and Glory on Wall Street: The Fall of the House of Lehman*. Harmondsworth, UK: Penguin Books, 1986.

Bar-Eli, M., S. Avugosa, and M. Raab. "Twenty Years of 'Hot Hand' Research: Review and Critique." *Psychology of Sport and Exercise* 7, no. 6 (2006).

Barkow, Jerome H., Leda Cosmides, and John Tooby. *The Adapted Mind: Evolutionary Psychology and the Generation of Culture*. New York: Oxford University Press, 1992.

Barr, Alfred H. *Picasso: Fifty Years of His Art*. New York: Museum of Modern Art, 1946.

Becker, G., and K. Murphy. "A Theory of Rational Addiction." *Journal of Political Economy* 96, no. 4 (1988), pp. 675–700.

Berlin, Isaiah. *Four Essays on Liberty*. London: Oxford University Press, 1969.

Berlin, Isaiah. *The Fox and the Hedgehog: An Essay on Tolstoy's View of History*. London: Weidenfeld & Nicolson, 1953.

Berlin, Isaiah. "My Intellectual Path." *New York Review of Books* XLV, no. 8 (1998).

Bevan, Judi. *The Rise and Fall of Marks and Spencer: And How It Rose Again*. London: Profile Books, 2001.

Bilefsky, D., and A. Raghavan. "How ABB Tumbled Back Down to Earth." *Wall Street Journal* (Europe), January 23, 2003.

Binmore, Ken. *Game Theory and the Social Contract*. Vol. 1, *Playing Fair*. Cambridge, MA: MIT Press, 1994.

Blastland, Michael, and Andrew Dilnot. *The Tiger That Isn't: Seeing Through a World of Numbers*. London: Profile, 2007.

Borges, Jorge Luis. *A Universal History of Infamy*. Harmondsworth, UK: Penguin, 1975.

Brand, Paul, and Philip Yancey. *The Gift of Pain: Why We Hurt and What We Can Do About It*. Grand Rapids, MI: Zondervan, 1997.

Brickman, P., D. Coates, and R. Janoff-Bulman. "Lottery Winners and Accident Victims: Is Happiness Relative?" *Journal of Personality and Social Psychology* 36, no. 8 (1978), pp. 917–27.

Bruck, Connie. *The Predators' Ball: The Inside Story of Drexel Burnham and the Rise of the Junk Bond Raider*. London: Penguin, 1989.

Byrne, John A. *The Whiz Kids: The Founding Fathers of American Business—and the Legacy They Left Us*. New York: Bantam Doubleday Dell, 1993.

Cahoone, Lawrence E., ed. *From Modernism to Postmodernism: An Anthology*. Edinburgh: Wiley-Blackwell, 2003.

Carnegie, Andrew. *The Gospel of Wealth and Other Timely Essays*. 1889. Reprint edited by Edward Chase Kirkland. Cambridge, MA: Belknap, 1962.

Caro, Robert A. *The Power Broker: Robert Moses and the Fall of New York*. New York: Vintage Books, 1975.

Caro, Robert A. *The Years of Lyndon Johnson*. London: Bodley Head, 1990.

Carré, M., T. Asai, T. Akatsuka, and S. J. Haake. "The Curve Kick of a Football I: Impact with the Foot." *Sports Engineering* 5, no. 4 (2002).

Carré, M., T. Asai, T. Akatsuka, and S. J. Haake. "The Curve Kick of a Football II: Flight Through the Air." *Sports Engineering* 5, no. 4 (2002).

Chamberlain, Neville. "Peace in Our Time." Speech to House of Commons, September 30, 1938.

Chernow, Ron. *Titan: The Life of John D. Rockefeller, Sr.* London: Little, Brown, 1998.

Christensen, C. R., J. W. Rosenblum, and C. B. Weigle. "Prelude Corporation." *Harvard Business School Case Studies*, August 1, 1972.

Churchill, Winston. "Upon the Death of Neville Chamberlain." Speech to House of Commons, November 12, 1940.

Clark, Ronald W. *Benjamin Franklin: A Biography*. London: Weidenfeld & Nicolson, 1983.

Collins, Jim. *Good to Great*. London: Random House Business Books, 2001.

Collins, Jim. *How the Mighty Fall*. London: Random House Business Books, 2009.

Collins, Jim, and Jerry I. Porras. *Built to Last: Successful Habits of Visionary Companies*. London: Random House Business Books, 2000.

Conniff, Richard. *The Natural History of the Rich*. New York: Norton, 2002.

Conrad, Joseph. *Typhoon and Other Stories*. London: William Heinemann, 1903.

Cornford, Francis M. *Microcosmographia Academica*. Cambridge: Bowes & Bowes, 1908.

Csikszentmihalyi, Mihalyi. *Flow: The Psychology of Optimal Experience*. New York: Harper Perennial, 1990.

Csikszentmihalyi, Mihalyi. *Living Well*. London: Weidenfeld & Nicolson, 1997.

Cullerne Brown, Matthew. *Art Under Stalin*. Oxford: Phaidon Press, 1991.

Cunningham, Lawrence A. *The Essays of Warren Buffett: Lessons for Investors and Managers*. Singapore: John Wiley & Sons, 2002.

Damasio, Antonio. *Descartes' Error: Emotion, Reason, and the Human Brain*. New York: Quill, 2000.

Darwin, Charles. *The Autobiography of Charles Darwin*. Edited by Nora Barlow. London: Collins, 1958.

Dawkins, Richard. *The Blind Watchmaker*. Harlow, UK: Longman Scientific & Technical, 1986.

Dawkins, Richard. *The Selfish Gene*. Oxford: Oxford University Press, 1989.

Dickinson, Emily. *Emily Dickinson*. Edited by L. Dickey. New York: Dell, 1960.

Dolnick, Edward. *The Forger's Spell: A True Story of Vermeer, Nazis, and the Greatest Art Hoax of the Twentieth Century*. New York: HarperCollins, 2008.

Dreyfus, Hubert L. *What Computers Still Can't Do*. Cambridge, MA: MIT Press, 1992.

Dunlap, Albert J., with Bob Andelman. *Mean Business: How I Save Bad Companies and Make Good Companies Great*. New York: Fireside, 1996.

Durham, William H. *Coevolution: Genes, Culture, and Human Diversity*. Stanford, CA: Stanford University Press, 1991.

Edmonds, David, and John Eidinow. *Bobby Fischer Goes to War*. London: Faber & Faber, 2004.

Elster, Jon. *Ulysses Unbound*. Cambridge: Cambridge University Press, 2000.

Ferguson, Adam. *An Essay on the History of Civil Society*. 1767. Reprint, Edinburgh: Edinburgh University Press, 1966.

Fitzgerald, F. Scott. "The Crack-up." *Esquire*, February 1936.

Fortune International. "Top 100 Most Admired Companies." Various years.

Foster, R. F. *The Irish Story: Telling Tales and Making It Up in Ireland*. London: Allen Lane, 2001.

Foster, R. F. *Modern Ireland*. London: Penguin, 1989.

Franklin, Benjamin. *The Autobiography of Benjamin Franklin*. 1791. Reprint, New Haven, CT: Yale University Press, 1964.

Frey, Bruno S., and Alois Stutzer. *Happiness and Economics: How the Economy and Institutions Affect Human Well-Being*. Princeton, NJ: Princeton University Press, 2002.

Fukuyama, Francis. *America at the Crossroads: Democracy, Power and the Neoconservative Legacy*. New Haven, CT: Yale University Press, 2006.

Fukuyama, Francis. *The End of History and the Last Man*. London: Free Press, 1992.

Fukuyama, F., D. Coats, and R. Janoff-Bulman. "The End of History." *National Interest* 15 (summer 1989).

Gale, J., K. G. Binmore, and L. Samuelson. "Learning to Be Imperfect: The Ultimatum Game." *Games and Economic Behavior* 8, no. 1 (1995).

Gardner, Chris, with Quincy Troupe. *The Pursuit of Happyness*. New York: Amistad, 2006.

Gardner, Helen, ed. *The New Oxford Book of English Verse, 1250–1950*. Oxford: Oxford University Press, 1972.

Gigerenzer, Gerd, et al. *Simple Heuristics That Make Us Smart*. New York: Oxford University Press, 1999.

Gilovich, T., R. Vallone, and A. Tversky. "The Hot Hand in Basketball: On the Misperception of Random Sequences." *Cognitive Psychology* vol. 17 (1985).

Gintis, Herbert. *Game Theory Evolving*. 2nd ed. Princeton, NJ: Princeton University Press, 2009.

Gladwell, Malcolm. *Blink*. London: Allen Lane, 2005.

Gombrich, Ernst H. *The Story of Art*. Oxford: Phaidon Press, 1978.

Goodhart, C. A. E. "Monetary Relationships: A View from Threadneedle Street."
    Reserve Bank of Australia, *Papers in Monetary Economics* 1 (1975).

Graham, Benjamin, and David Dodd. *Security Analysis*. New York: McGraw Hill, 1951.

Guerrera, F., "Welch Condemns Share Price Focus." *Financial Times*, March 13, 2009.

Haidt, Jonathan. *The Happiness Hypothesis*. London: Arrow Books, 2006.

Halberstam, David. *The Reckoning*. London: Bloomsbury, 1987.

Hamermesh, Richard G. *Making Strategy Work*. New York: John Wiley & Sons, 1986.

Hammer, Michael, and James Champy. *Reengineering the Corporation: A Manifesto for
    Business Revolution*. London: Nicholas Brearley, 1995.

Hammond, J. S., R. L. Keeny, and H. Raiffa. "Even Swaps: A Rational Method
    for Making Trade Offs." *Harvard Business Review* 76, no. 2 (Mar.–Apr. 1998),
    pp. 137–50.

Hawkes, J. G., and J. Francisco-Ortega. "The Early History of the Potato in Europe."
    Euphytica 70, no. 1–2 (Jan. 1993).

Hayek, Friedrich von. *Law, Legislation and Liberty*. Vol. 1, *Rules and Order*. Chicago:
    University of Chicago Press, 1973.

Highfield, R. "The Mind-Bending Genius of Beckham." *Daily Telegraph*, May 21, 2002.

Hinz, Berthold. *Art in the Third Reich*. Oxford: Blackwell, 1980.

HM Treasury. *Microeconomic Reform in Britain: Delivering Opportunities for All*. Edited by
    E. Balls, G. O'Donnell, and J. Grice. Houndmills, UK: Palgrave Macmillan, 2004.

Horton, John, and Susan Mendus. *After MacIntyre: Critical Perspectives on the Work of
    Alasdair MacIntyre*. Cambridge: Polity, 1994.

Hume, David. *Essays: Moral, Political, Literary*. 1777. Reprint, ed. Eugene F. Miller,
    Indianapolis: Liberty Classics, 1985.

Hutton, Will. *The World We're In*. London: Little, Brown, 2002.

Huxley, Aldous. *Brave New World*. London: Chatto and Windus, 1932.

ICI. "Annual Report." 1990.

ICI. "Annual Report." 1997.

Jacobs, Jane. *The Death and Life of Great American Cities*. Harmondsworth, UK:
    Penguin, 1965.

Jencks, Charles. *The Language of Post-Modern Architecture*. London: Academy
    Editions, 1984.

Jenkins, Roy. *Churchill*. London: Macmillan, 2001.

JPMorgan and Reuters. *RiskMetrics—Technical Document*. 4th ed. New York: Morgan
    Guaranty Trust Company of New York, 1996.

Kahneman, Daniel, Ed Diener, and Norbert Schwarz. *Well-being: The Foundations of
    Hedonic Psychology*. New York: Russell Sage Foundation, 2003.

Kahneman, D., and A. Tversky. "Prospect Theory: An Analysis of Decisions Under
    Risk." *Econometrica* vol. 47 (1979).

Kaplan, Robert S., and David P. Norton. *The Balanced Scorecard: Translating Strategy into
    Action*. Boston: Harvard Business School Press, 1996.

Kay, John. *The Truth About Markets*. London: Penguin Allen Lane, 2003.

Kay, John A., Jeremy Edwards, and Colin P. Mayer. *The Economic Analysis of Accounting
    Profitability*. Oxford: Oxford University Press, 1987.

Keats, John. *Poems by John Keats*. London: Methuen, n.d.

Kelvin, Lord. *Popular Lectures and Addresses*. Vol. 1. London: Macmillan, 1891.

Kets de Vries, M. "Leaders Who Make a Difference." *European Management Journal* 14, no. 5 (Oct. 1996).

Keynes, John Maynard. *The Collected Writings of John Maynard Keynes*. Vol. X. London: Macmillan Press, 1972.

Kilgore, B. M. "Origin and History of Wildland Fire Use in the U.S. National Park System." *George Wright Forum* 24, no. 3 (2007).

Kiple, Kenneth F., and Kriemhild Coneè Ornelas, eds. *Cambridge World History of Food*. Vol. 1. Cambridge: Cambridge University Press, 2000.

Klein, Gary A. *Sources of Power: How People Make Decisions*. Cambridge, MA: MIT Press, 1998.

Langley, Monica. *Tearing Down the Walls*. New York: Simon & Schuster, 2003.

Layard, Richard. *Happiness: Lessons from a New Science*. London: Allen Lane, 2005.

Le Corbusier. *The Radiant City*. London: Faber & Faber, 1964.

Le Corbusier. *Toward a New Architecture*. London: Architectural Press, 1982.

Lenin, Vladimir Ilyich. *Essential Works of Lenin: What Is to Be Done?* 1902. Reprint, New York: Dover, 1987.

Levitt, Theodore. "Marketing Myopia." *Harvard Business Review* 38, no. 4 (July–Aug. 1960).

Lewis, Michael. *Liar's Poker: Two Cities, True Greed*. London: Hodder & Stoughton, 1989.

Lindblom, Charles. "The Science of 'Muddling Through.'" *Public Administration Review* 19, no. 2 (1959).

Lindblom, Charles. "Still Muddling, Not Yet Through." *Public Administration Review* 39, no. 6 (1979).

Loewenstein, G. "Because It Is There: The Challenge of Mountaineering . . . for Utility Theory." *Kyklos International Review for Social Sciences* 52, no. 3 (1999).

Loewenstein, Roger. *Buffett: The Making of an American Capitalist*. New York: Broadway Books, 1995.

Lopez, Jonathan. *The Man Who Made Vermeers: Unvarnishing the Legend of Master Forger Han van Meegeren*. New York: Mariner Books, 2008.

MacIntyre, Alasdair. *After Virtue: A Study in Moral Theory*. 2nd ed. London: Gerald Duckworth, 1994.

McNamara, Robert S., with Brian VanDeMark. *In Retrospect: The Tragedy and Lessons of Vietnam*. New York: Vintage, 1996.

Malabre, Alfred L. *Lost Prophets: An Insider's History of Modern Economists*. Boston, MA: Harvard Business School Press, 1994.

Markon, J., and R. Merle. "Ex-Boeing CFO Pleads Guilty in Druyun Case." *Washington Post*, November 16, 2004.

Marks & Spencer. "Annual Report." 1998.

Messner, Reinhold. *The Crystal Horizon: Everest: The First Solo Ascent*. Ramsbury, UK: Crowood Press, 1989.

Meyer, M. "From a Champ to a Chump." *Newsweek*, July 26, 1993.

Mill, John Stuart. *Autobiography*. 1873. Reprint, London: Penguin, 1989.

Mill, John Stuart. *Utilitarianism*. 1863. Reprint, Charleston, SC: BiblioBazaar, 2008.

Mintzberg, Henry. *The Rise and Fall of Strategic Planning*. Hemel Hempstead, UK: Prentice Hall, 1994.

Morita, Aiko. *Made in Japan*. London: Collins, 1987.

Morris, A. E. J. *History of the Urban Form: Before the Industrial Revolutions*. 3rd ed. New York: Longman Scientific and Technical, 1994.

Myers, David G. *The Pursuit of Happiness: Who Is Happy and Why?* London: Aquarian Press, 1993.

Nakamoto, M., and D. Wighton. "Citigroup Chief Stays Bullish on Buy-outs." *Financial Times*, July 10, 2007.

Nettle, Daniel. *Happiness: The Science Behind Your Smile*. Oxford: Oxford University Press, 2005.

New York Times. "Climbing Mount Everest Is Work of Supermen." March 18, 1923.

Nocera, J. "Risk Management." *New York Times*, January 4, 2009.

Nozick, Robert. *Anarchy, State and Utopia*. Oxford: Blackwell, 1995.

Paley, William. *Natural Theology*. 1802. Reprint, Weybridge, UK: Hamilton, n.d.

Pandolfini, Bruce. *Kasparov and Deep Blue: The Historic Chess Match Between Man and Machine*. New York: Simon & Schuster, 1997.

Pascale, R. T. "Perspectives on Strategy: The Real Story Behind Honda's Success." *California Management Review* 26, no. 3 (1984).

Plutarch. *Plutarch's Lives*. London: William Heinemann, 1948.

Polanyi, Michael. *The Tacit Dimension*. Gloucester, MA: Peter Smith, 1983.

Porter, M. E., and K. Schwab. *The Global Competitiveness Report 2008–2009*. Geneva: World Economic Forum, 2008.

Quiller-Couch, Arthur, ed. *Oxford Book of English Verse 1250–1918*. 1919. Reprint, Oxford: Clarendon Press, 1961.

Ricks, Christopher, ed. *The Oxford Book of English Verse*. Oxford: Oxford University Press, 1999.

Ridley, Matt. *Origins of Virtue*. London: Penguin Science, 1998.

Roosevelt, Franklin Delano. *Looking Forward*. London: William Heinemann, 1933.

Rosenzweig, Philip M. *The Halo Effect*. New York: Free Press, 2007.

Rosenzweig, P., "What Do We Think Happened at ABB? Pitfalls in Research About Firm Performance." *International Journal of Management and Decision Making*, vol. 5, no. 4 (2004).

Rotella, Bob, with Bob Cullen. *Golf Is Not a Game of Perfect*. London: Pocket Books, 2004.

Ryan, R., and E. Deci. "On Happiness and Human Potential." *Annual Review of Psychology* 52 (2001).

Ryff, C. D. "Happiness Is Everything, or Is It?" *Journal of Personality and Social Psychology*, vol. 57, no. 6 (1989).

Saint-Gobain. "Annual Report 2008."

Samuelson, P. A. "Altruism as a Problem Involving Group Versus Individual Selection in Economics and Biology." *American Economic Review* 83, no. 2 (May 1998).

Samuelson, Paul. *Foundations of Economic Analysis*. Cambridge, MA: Harvard University Press, 1966.

Schroder, Alice. *The Snowball: Warren Buffett and the Business of Life*. London: Bloomsbury, 2008.

Scott, James. *Seeing Like a State*. New Haven, CT: Yale University Press, 1999.

Securities and Exchange Commission. "Enforcement Proceedings." *SEC News Digest* 2002-171 (September 4, 2002).

Sen, A. "Internal Consistency of Choice." *Econometrica*, vol. 61, no. 3 (May 1993).

Sennett, Richard. *The Craftsman*. London: Allen Lane, 2008.

Shiva Kumar, A. K., and S. Fukuda-Parr, eds. *Handbook of Human Development: Concepts, Measures, and Policies*. New Delhi: Oxford University Press, 2009.

Sieff, Israel M. *Memoirs*. London: Weidenfeld & Nicolson, 1970.

Simon, H. A., and A. Newell. "Heuristic Problem Solving: The Next Advance in Operations Research." *Operations Research* 6, no. 1 (Jan.–Feb. 1958).

Singh, Simon. *Fermat's Last Theorem*. London: Fourth Estate, 1997.

Smith, Adam. *An Inquiry into the Nature and Causes of the Wealth of Nations*. 1776. Abridged, with commentary, Indianapolis and Cambridge: Hackett Publishing, 1993.

Smith, Ed. *What Sport Tells Us About Life*. London: Penguin, 2008.

Sobel, Robert. *The Rise and Fall of the Conglomerate Kings*. New York: Stein and Day, 1984.

Solomon, Robert C. *Ethics and Excellence*. New York: Oxford University Press, 1994.

Soros, George. *The Alchemy of Finance*. Hoboken, NJ: John Wiley & Sons, 2003.

Sparkes, Boyden, and Samuel Taylor Moore. *Hetty Green: A Woman Who Loved Money*. London: William Heinemann, 1930.

Stern, Carl W., and George Stalk, eds. *Perspectives on Strategy from the Boston Consulting Group*. New York: John Wiley, 1998.

Stewart, James B. *Den of Thieves*. New York: Simon & Schuster, 1991.

Stork, David G., ed. *Hal's Legacy: 2001's Computer as a Dream and Reality*. Cambridge, MA: MIT Press, 1997.

Strauss, Maurice B. *Familiar Medical Quotations*. London: J & A Churchill, 1968.

Sunstein, Cass R. *Legal Reasoning and Political Conflict*. Oxford: Oxford University Press, 1996.

Taleb, Nassim Nicholas. *Fooled by Randomness*. New York: Texere, 2001.

Tetlock, Philip E. *Expert Political Judgment: How Good Is It? How Can We Know?* Princeton, NJ: Princeton University Press, 2005.

Tolstoy, Leo. *War and Peace*. 1869. Reprint, Ware, UK: Wordsworth Editions, 1993.

Tomlinson, R., and P. Hjelt. "Dethroning Percy Barnevik." *Fortune International* (Europe), April 1, 2002.

Trump, Donald J., with Tony Schwartz. *Trump: The Art of the Deal*. New York: Warner Books, 1987.

Tucker, Spencer C., ed. *Encyclopedia of the Vietnam War*. Santa Barbara, CA: ABC-CLIO, 1998.

Tversky, A., and D. Kahneman. "Belief in the Law of Small Numbers." *Psychological Bulletin* vol. 76 (1971).

Tversky, A., and D. Kahneman. "The Framing of Decisions and the Psychology of Choice." *Science* no. 211 (1981).

United Nations Development Programme. *Human Development Report*. New York: Palgrave Macmillan, various years.

U.S. Congress. House of Representatives. Committee on Oversight and Government Reform. *Transcript of Hearing (Richard Fuld)*. October 6, 2008. Hearing on Effects and Causes of the Bankruptcy of Lehman Brothers, 110th Congress, 2nd session.

U.S. National Park Service. *The Yellowstone Fires of 1988*. 2008.

Vasari, Giorgio. *Lives of the Painters, Sculptors, and Architects*. Vol. I. London: George Bell & Sons, 1878.

Walton, Sam, with John Huey. *Made in America: My Story*. New York: Bantam, 1993.

Welch, Jack. "Jack Welch Elaborates: Shareholder Value." *BusinessWeek*, March 16, 2009.

Welch, Jack, with John A. Byrne. *Jack: Straight from the Gut*. London: Headline, 2003.

Weston, Richard. *Modernism*. London: Phaidon Press, 1996.

Whately, Elizabeth Jane. *Life and Correspondence of Richard Whately, D.D.* Vol. II. London: Longmans, Green, 1866.

Whitman, Walt. "Song of Myself." In *Leaves of Grass*. 1855. Reprint, Hertfordshire, UK: Wordsworth Editions, 2006.

Wilde, Oscar. *The Picture of Dorian Gray*. 1890. Reprint, Mineola, NY: Dover, 1993.

Wilke, A., and H. C. Barrett. "The Hot Hand Phenomenon as a Cognitive Adaptation to Clumped Resources." *Evolution and Human Behavior* 30, no. 3 (2009).

W. S. M., "The Origin of Our Potato." *Nature*, May 6, 1886.

Zumbach, G., "A Gentle Introduction to the RM 2006 Methodology." RiskMetrics Working Paper, September 2006.

Index

Printed in the United States
by Baker & Taylor Publisher Services